Meeting the Needs

of Your Most Able Pupils:

HISTORY

Other titles in the series

Meeting the Needs of Your Most Able Pupils: Art
Kim Earle
1 84312 331 2
978 1 84312 331 6

Meeting the Needs of Your Most Able Pupils: Design and Technology
Louise T. Davies
1 84312 330 4
978 1 84312 330 9

Meeting the Needs of Your Most Able Pupils: Mathematics
Lynne McClure and Jennifer Piggott
1 84312 328 2
978 1 84312 328 6

Meeting the Needs of Your Most Able Pupils: Music
Jonathan Savage
1 84312 347 9
978 1 84312 347 7

Meeting the Needs of Your Most Able Pupils: Physical Education and Sport
David Morley and Richard Bailey
1 84312 334 7
978 1 84312 334 7

Meeting the Needs
of Your Most Able Pupils:
HISTORY

Steven Barnes

Routledge
Taylor & Francis Group

LONDON AND NEW YORK

First published 2007 by
Routledge
2 Park Square, Milton Park, Abingdon, Oxon OX14 4RN

Simultaneously published in the USA and Canada by
Routledge
270 Madison Ave, New York, NY 10016

Routledge is an imprint of Taylor & Francis, an informa business

British Library Cataloguing in Publication data
A catalogue record for this book is available from the British Library

Library of Congress Cataloging in Publication Data
A catalog record has been requested

ISBN 13: 978 1 84312 287 6 (pbk)
ISBN 13: 978 0 203 93527 9 (ebk)
ISBN 10: 1 84312 287 1 (pbk)
ISBN 10: 0 203 93527 6 (ebk)

Series production editors: Sarah Fish and Andrew Welsh
Typeset by Servis Filmsetting Ltd, Manchester
Printed and bound in Great Britain
by Bell & Bain Ltd, Glasgow

Contents

Acknowledgements

There are a large number of people that helped the author in writing this book. First of all to Gwen Goodhew and Linda Evans; colleagues at CfBT in Lincolnshire, particularly Pat Hollingworth, Neil Triggs and Tim Lomas who have never failed to be stimulating, thought-provoking and willing to ask awkward questions. Nick Sparks has been an inspiration. His deceptively simple questions would leave colleagues musing and thinking for a long time. He will be missed as he transfers to Manchester University from the National Strategy.

Above all this book owes a huge amount of debt to my wife Tasha and son Rowan. Tasha has been a support and confidante. Those who know her will realise how much of this book is due to her.

Contributors to the series

The author

Steven Barnes is a former head of history at a secondary school and Secondary Strategy consultant for the School Improvement Service in Lincolnshire. He has written history exemplifications for Assessment for Learning for the Secondary National Strategy. He is now an assistant head with responsibility for teaching and learning for a school in Lincolnshire.

Series editor

Gwen Goodhew's many and varied roles within the field of gifted and talented education have included school G&T coordinator, director of Wirral Able Children Centre, Knowsley Excellence in Cities (EiC) G&T coordinator, member of the DfES G&T Advisory Group, teacher trainer and consultant. She has written and edited numerous reports and articles on the subject and co-authored *Providing for Able Children* with Linda Evans.

Other authors

Art

Kim Earle is a former secondary head of art and design and is currently an able pupils and arts consultant for St Helens. She has been a member of DfES steering groups, is an Artsmark validator, a subject editor for G&TWISE and a practising designer jeweller and enameller.

Design and Technology

During the writing of the book **Louise T. Davies** was a part-time subject adviser for design and technology at the QCA (Qualifications and Curriculum Authority), and part of the KS3 National Strategy team for the D&T programme. She has authored over 40 D&T books and award-winning multimedia resources. She is currently deputy chief executive of the Design and Technology Association.

Mathematics

Lynne McClure is an independent consultant in the field of mathematics education and G&T. She works with teachers and students in schools all over the

UK and abroad as well as Warwick, Cambridge, Oxford Brookes and Edinburgh Universities. Lynne edits several maths and education journals.

Jennifer Piggott is a lecturer in mathematics enrichment and communication technology at Cambridge University. She is Director of the NRICH mathematics project and is part of the eastern region coordination team for the NCETM (National Centre for Excellence in the Teaching of Mathematics). Jennifer is an experienced mathematics and ICT teacher.

Music

Jonathan Savage is a senior lecturer in music education at the Institute of Education, Manchester Metropolitan University. Until 2001 he was head of music at Debenham High School, an 11–16 comprehensive school in Suffolk. He is a co-author of a new resource introducing computer game sound design to the Key Stage 3 curriculum (www.sound2game.net) and managing director of UCan.tv (www.ucan.tv), a company specialising in the production of educational software and hardware. When not doing all of this, he is busy parenting four very musically talented children!

Physical Education and Sport

David Morley has taught physical education in a number of secondary schools. He is currently senior lecturer in physical education at Leeds Metropolitan University and the director of the national DfES-funded 'Development in PE' project which is part of the Gifted and Talented strand of the PE, School Sport and Club Links (PESSCL) project. He is also a member of the team responsible for developing resources for national Multi-skill Clubs and is the founder and director of the Carnegie Regional Multi-skill Camp held at Leeds Met Carnegie.

Richard Bailey is professor of pedagogy at Roehampton University, having previously worked at Reading and Leeds Metropolitan University, and at Canterbury Christ Church University where he was director of the Centre for Physical Education Research. He is a well-known author and speaker on physical education, sport and education.

Online content on the Routledge website

The online material accompanying this book may be used by the purchasing individual/organisation only. The files may be amended to suit particular situations, or individual learning needs, and printed out for use by the purchaser. The material can be accessed at www.routledge.com/education/fultonresources.asp

01 Institutional quality standards in gifted and talented education
02 Auditing provision for the most able students in history at Key Stages 3–4
03 High ability or potential – a history checklist
04 Coaching
05 Sample lesson plan (Year 7) – The Battle of Hastings
06 Story sheet – The Norman Conquest
07 Sample lesson plan (Year 9) – The Industrial Revolution
08 Concept map example
09 Sample lesson plan (Year 9) – The assassination of Archduke Franz Ferdinand
10 Counterfactual reasoning example
11 Sample lesson plan (Year 10) – Cholera
12 Mystery cards – Why didn't Mr Higgins' men die of cholera?
13 Sample lesson plan (Year 10) – South Africa since 1948
14 Where were the highs and lows of Apartheid between 1950 and 1994?
15 Lifeline cards – South Africa

www.routledge.com/education

Introduction

Who should use this book?

This book is for all teachers of history working with Key Stage 3 and Key Stage 4 pupils. It will be relevant to teachers working within the full spectrum of schools, from highly selective establishments to comprehensive and secondary modern schools as well as some special schools. Its overall objective is to provide a practical resource that heads of department, gifted and talented coordinators, leading teachers for gifted and talented education and classroom teachers can use to develop a coherent approach to provision for their most able pupils.

Why is it needed?

School populations differ greatly and pupils considered very able in one setting might not stand out in another. Nevertheless, whatever the general level of ability within a school, there has been a tendency to plan and provide for the middle range, to modify for those who are struggling and to leave the most able to 'get on with it'. This has meant that the most able have:

- not been sufficiently challenged and stimulated

- underachieved

- been unaware of what they might be capable of achieving

- been unaware of what they need to do to achieve at the highest level

- not had high enough ambitions and aspirations

- sometimes become disaffected.

How will this book help teachers?

This book and its accompanying website will, through its combination of practical ideas, materials for photocopying or downloading, and case studies:

- help teachers of history to focus on the top 5–10% of the ability range in their particular school and to find ways of providing for these pupils, both within and beyond the classroom

- equip them with strategies and ideas to support exceptionally able pupils, i.e. those in the top 5% nationally.

Terminology

Since there is confusion about the meaning of the words 'gifted' and 'talented', the terms 'more able', 'most able' and 'exceptionally able' will generally be used in this series.

When 'gifted' and 'talented' are used, the definitions provided by the Department for Education and Skills (DfES) in its Excellence in Cities programme will apply. That is:

- **gifted** pupils are the most academically able in a school. This ability might be general or specific to a particular subject area, such as mathematics.

- **talented** pupils are those with high ability or potential in art, music, performing arts or sport.

The two groups together should form 5–10% of any school population.

There are, of course, some pupils who are both gifted and talented. Examples that come to mind are the budding physicist who plays the violin to a high standard in his spare time, or the pupil with high general academic ability who plays for the area football team.

This book is part of a series dealing with providing challenge for the most able secondary age pupils in a range of subjects. It is likely that some of the books in the series might also contain ideas that would be relevant to teachers of history.

CHAPTER 1

Our more able pupils – the national scene

- Making good provision for the most able – what's in it for schools?
- National initiatives since 1997
- *Every Child Matters* and the Children Act 2004
- *Higher Standards, Better Schools for All* – Education White Paper, October 2005
- Self-evaluation and inspection
- Resources for teachers and parents of more able pupils

Today's gifted pupils are tomorrow's social, intellectual, economic and cultural leaders and their development cannot be left to chance.

(Deborah Eyre, director of the National Academy for Gifted and Talented Youth, 2004)

The debate about whether to make special provision for the most able pupils in secondary schools ran its course during the last decade of the twentieth century. Explicit provision to meet their learning needs is now considered neither elitist nor a luxury. From an inclusion angle these pupils must have the same chances as others to develop their potential to the full. We know from international research that focusing on the needs of the most able changes teachers' perceptions of the needs of all their pupils, and there follows a consequential rise in standards. But for teachers who are not convinced by the inclusion or school improvement arguments, there is a much more pragmatic reason for meeting the needs of able pupils. Of course, it is preferable that colleagues share a common willingness to address the needs of the most able, but if they don't, it can at least be pointed out that, quite simply, it is something that all teachers are now required to do, not an optional extra.

All schools should seek to create an atmosphere in which to excel is not only acceptable but desirable.

(*Excellence in Schools* – DfEE 1997)

High achievement is determined by 'the school's commitment to inclusion and the steps it takes to ensure that every pupil does as well as possible'.

(*Handbook for Inspecting Secondary Schools* – Ofsted, 2003)

A few years ago, efforts to raise standards in schools concentrated on getting as many pupils as possible over the Level 5 hurdle at the end of Key Stage 3 and over the 5 A*–C grades hurdle at GCSE. Resources were pumped into borderline pupils and the most able were not, on the whole, considered a cause for concern. The situation has changed dramatically in the last nine years with schools being expected to set targets for A*s and As and to show added value by helping pupils entering the school with high SATs scores to achieve Levels 7 and beyond, if supporting data suggests that that is what is achievable. Early recognition of high potential and the setting of curricular targets are at last addressing the lack of progress demonstrated by many able pupils in Year 7 and more attention is being paid to creating a climate in which learning can flourish. But there is a push for even more support for the most able through the promotion of personalised learning.

> The goal is that five years from now: gifted and talented students progress in line with their ability rather than their age; schools inform parents about tailored provision in an annual school profile; curricula include a gifted and talented dimension and at 14–19 there is more stretch and differentiation at the top end, so no matter what your talent it will be engaged; and the effect of poverty on achievement is reduced, because support for high-ability students from poorer backgrounds enables them to thrive.
>
> (Speech at National Academy for Gifted and Talented Youth – David Miliband, Minister for State for School Standards, May 2004)

It is hoped that this book, with the others in this series, will help to accelerate these changes.

Making good provision for the most able – what's in it for schools?

Schools and/or subject departments often approach provision for the most able pupils with some reluctance because they imagine a lot of extra work for very little reward. In fact, the rewards of providing for these pupils are substantial.

- It can be very stimulating to the subject specialist to explore ways of developing approaches with enthusiastic and able students.

> Taking a serious look at what I should expect from the most able and then at how I should teach them has given my teaching a new lease of life. I feel so sorry for youngsters who were taught by me ten years ago. They must have been bored beyond belief. But then, to be quite honest, so was I.
>
> (Science teacher)

- Offering opportunities to tackle work in a more challenging manner often interests pupils whose abilities have gone unnoticed because they have not been motivated by a bland educational diet.

> Some of the others were invited to an after-school maths club. When I heard what they were doing, it sounded so interesting that I asked the maths teacher if I could go too. She was a bit doubtful at first because I have messed about a lot but she agreed to take me on trial. I'm one of her star pupils now and she reckons I'll easily get an A*. I still find some of the lessons really slow and boring but I don't mess around – well, not too much.
>
> (Year 10 boy)

- When pupils are engaged by the work they are doing motivation, attainment and discipline improve.

> You don't need to be gifted to work out that the work we do is much more interesting and exciting. It's made others want to be like us.
>
> (Comment of a student involved in an extension programme for the most able)

- Schools identified as very good by Ofsted generally have good provision for their most able students.

> If you are willing to deal effectively with the needs of able pupils you will raise the achievement of all pupils.
>
> (Mike Tomlinson, former director of Ofsted)

- The same is true of individual departments in secondary schools. All those considered to be very good have spent time developing a sound working approach that meets the needs of their most able pupils.

> The department creates a positive atmosphere by its organisation, display and the way that students are valued. Learning is generally very good and often excellent throughout the school. The teachers' high expectations permeate the atmosphere and are a significant factor in raising achievement. These expectations are reflected in the curriculum which has depth and students are able and expected to experience difficult problems in all year groups.
>
> (Mathematics Department, Hamstead Hall School, Birmingham; Ofsted 2003)

National initiatives since 1997

In 1997, the new government demonstrated its commitment to gifted and talented education by setting up a Gifted and Talented Advisory Group (GTAG). Since then there has been a wide range of government and government-funded initiatives that have, either directly or indirectly, impacted on our most able pupils and their teachers. Details of some can be found below. Others that relate to history will be found later in this book.

Excellence in Cities

In an attempt to deal with the chronic underachievement of able pupils in inner city areas, Excellence in Cities (EiC) was launched in 1999. This was a very ambitious, well-funded programme with many different strands. In the first place it concentrated on secondary age pupils but work was extended into the primary sector in many areas. Provision for gifted and talented students was one of the strands.

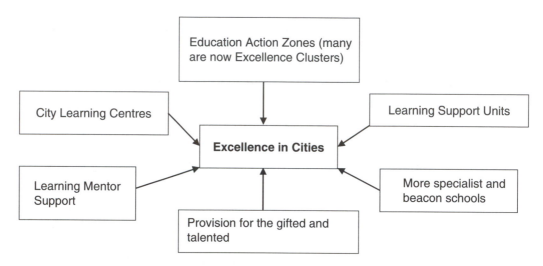

Strands in the Excellence in Cities initiative

EiC schools were expected to:

- develop a whole-school policy for their most able pupils

- appoint a gifted and talented coordinator with sufficient time to fulfil the role

- send the coordinator on a national training programme run by Oxford Brookes University

- identify 5–10% of pupils in each year group as their gifted and talented cohort, the gifted being the academically able and the talented being those with latent or obvious ability in PE, sport, music, art or the performing arts

- provide an appropriate programme of work both within the school day and beyond

- set 'aspirational' targets both for the gifted and talented cohort as a whole and for individual pupils

- work with other schools in a 'cluster' to provide further support for these pupils

- work with other agencies, such as Aimhigher, universities, businesses and private sector schools, to enhance provision and opportunities for these pupils.

Funding changes have meant that schools no longer receive dedicated EiC money through local authorities but the lessons learned from EiC have been influential in developing a national approach to gifted and talented education. **All** schools are now expected to adopt similar strategies to ensure that the needs of their most able students are met.

Excellence Clusters

Although EiC was set up initially in the main urban conurbations, other hot spots of underachievement and poverty were also identified and Excellence Clusters were established. For example, Ellesmere Port, Crewe and Barrow-in-Furness are pockets of deprivation, with major social problems and significant underachievement, in otherwise affluent areas. Excellence Clusters have been established in these three places and measures are being taken to improve provision for the most able pupils. The approach is similar to that used in Excellence in Cities areas.

Aimhigher

Aimhigher is another initiative of the Department for Education and Skills (DfES) working in partnership with the Higher Education Funding Council for England (HEFCE). Its remit is to widen participation in UK higher education, particularly among students from groups that do not have a tradition of going to university, such as some ethnic minorities, the disabled and those from poorer homes. Both higher education institutions and secondary schools have Aimhigher coordinators who work together to identify pupils who would benefit from additional support and to plan a programme of activities. Opportunities are likely to include:

- mentoring, including e-mentoring
- residential summer schools
- visits to different campuses and university departments
- masterclasses
- online information for students and parents
- advice on the wide range of financial and other support available to disadvantaged students.

One national Aimhigher project, Higher Education Gateway, is specifically targeted on gifted and talented students from disadvantaged groups. More information can be found at www.aimhigher.ac.uk.

National Academy for Gifted and Talented Youth (NAGTY)

Government initiatives have not been confined to the most able pupils in deprived areas. In 2002, the National Academy for Gifted and Talented Youth was established at Warwick University. Its brief was to offer support to the most able 5% of the school population and their teachers and parents. It did this in a number of ways:

National Academy for Gifted and Talented Youth		
Student Academy	**Professional Academy**	**Expertise Centre**
• Summer schools including link-ups with CTY in USA. • Outreach courses in a wide range of subjects at universities and other venues across the country. • Online activities – currently maths, classics, ethics, philosophy.	• Continuing professional development for teachers. • A PGCE+ programme for trainee teachers. • Ambassador School Programme to disseminate good practice amongst schools.	• Leading research in gifted and talented education.

NAGTY worked closely with the DfES with the latter setting policy and NAGTY increasingly taking the lead in the practical application of this policy – a policy known as the English Model, which, as explained on NAGTY's website, is 'rooted in day-to-day classroom provision and enhanced by additional, more advanced opportunities offered both within school and outside of it'. NAGTY ceased operation in August 2007 and was replaced by the Young, Gifted and Talented Programme (see below).

The Young, Gifted & Talented Programme (YG&T)

In December 2006, the UK government announced the creation of a new programme in England, the National Programme for Gifted and Talented Education (NPGATE), to be managed by CfBT Education Trust and now known as the Young, Gifted & Talented Programme (YG&T). Among the changes proposed are:

- a much greater emphasis on school and local level provision

- the setting-up of Excellence Hubs – HEI-led partnerships to provide non-residential summer schools and a diverse range of outreach provision, including summer activities, weekend events and online and blended learning models. There will be free places for the disadvantaged

- the appointment of gifted and talented leading teachers – one for each secondary school and each cluster of primary schools

- a national training programme for gifted and talented leading teachers organised by the national primary and secondary strategies.

Further information about YG&T can be found at www.dfes.gov.uk/ygt or www.cfbt.com.

Gifted and talented summer schools

Education authorities are encouraged to work in partnership with schools to run a number of summer schools (dependent on the size of the authority) for the most able pupils in Years 6–11. It is expected that there will be a particular emphasis on transition and that around 50 hours of tuition will be offered. Some schools and authorities run summer schools for up to ten days whilst others cover a shorter period and have follow-up sessions or even residential weekends later in the school year. Obviously the main aim is to challenge and stimulate these pupils but the DfES also hopes that:

- they will encourage teachers and advisers to adopt innovative teaching approaches
- teachers will continue to monitor these pupils over time
- where Year 6 pupils are involved, it will make secondary teachers aware of what they can achieve and raise their expectations of Year 7 pupils.

More can be found out about these summer schools at www.standards.dfes. gov.uk/giftedandtalented. Funding for them has now been incorporated into the school development grant.

Regional partnerships

When Excellence in Cities (EiC) was first introduced, gifted and talented strand coordinators from different EiC partnerships began to meet up with others in their regions to explore ways of working together so that the task would be more manageable and resources could be pooled. One of the most successful examples of cooperation was the Trans-Pennine Group that started up in the northwest. It began to organise training on a regional basis as well as masterclasses and other activities for some gifted and talented pupils. The success of this and other groups led to the setting-up of nine regional partnerships with initial support from NAGTY and finance from DfES. Each partnership had a steering group composed of representatives from local authorities, higher education institutions, regional organisations concerned with gifted and talented children and NAGTY. Each regional partnership organised professional training; sought to support schools and areas in greatest need; tried to ensure that all 11- to 19-year-olds who fell into the top 5% of the ability range were registered with NAGTY; provided opportunities for practitioner research and arranged challenging activities for pupils. Examples of all these can be found at www.nagty.ac.uk. Under the YG&T Programme, nine Excellence Hubs have been created to continue and expand the work of the regional partnerships.

Every Child Matters: *Change for Children* and the Children Act 2004

The likelihood of all children reaching their potential has always been hampered by the fragmented nature of agencies concerned with provision for them. Vital information held by an agency about a child's needs has often been kept back from other agencies, including schools. This has had a particularly negative impact on the disadvantaged, for example, looked-after children. In 2004, 57% of looked-after children left school without even one GCSE or GNVQ and only 6% achieved five or more good GCSEs (see national statistics at www.dfes.gov.uk/rsgateway/). This represents a huge waste of national talent as well as many personal tragedies.

The Children Act 2004 sought to overcome these problems by, amongst other things, requiring:

- local authorities to make arrangements to promote cooperation between agencies to ensure the well-being of all children

- all children's services to bear these five outcomes in mind when planning provision. Children should:

  - be healthy

  - stay safe

  - enjoy and achieve

  - make a positive contribution

  - achieve economic well-being.

There are major implications for schools in seeking to achieve these outcomes for their most able pupils, especially where there is deprivation and/or low aspiration:

- local authorities to appoint a director of children's services to coordinate education and social services

- each local authority to take on the role of corporate parent to promote the educational achievement of looked-after children. This should help to ensure that greater consideration is given to their education when changes in foster placements are being considered

- the setting-up of an integrated inspection regime to look at the totality of provision for children.

More information can be found at www.everychildmatters.gov.uk.

Higher Standards, Better Schools for All (Education White Paper, October 2005)

Although the thrust of this Education White Paper is to improve educational opportunities for all, there is no doubt that some proposals will particularly benefit the most able, especially those that are disadvantaged in some way.

- Pupils receiving free school meals will be able to get **free public transport** to any one of three secondary schools closest to their homes between two and six miles away. At present, such children have very little choice in secondary schooling because their parents cannot afford the fares. This measure will allow them access to schools that might be better able to cater for their particular strengths and needs.

- **The National Register of Gifted and Talented Learners** will record the top 5% of the nation's children, as identified by a wide range of measures, so that they can be tracked and supported throughout their school careers. At first, the focus will be on 11- to 19-year-olds but later identification will start at the age of 4. As a first step, in 2006 all secondary schools were asked to identify gifted and talented students in the school census. In reality, some authorities had already begun this monitoring process but making it a national priority will bring other schools and authorities up to speed.

- In line with new school managerial structures, **'leading teachers' of the gifted and talented** will take the place of gifted and talented coordinators. Training (optionally accredited) will be organised through the national strategies. Leading teachers will work closely with School Improvement Partners and local authority coordinators to implement gifted and talented improvement plans and undertake much of the work previously undertaken by school coordinators.

- **Additional training** in providing for gifted and talented pupils will be available to all schools.

- **A national programme of non-residential summer schools** will be organised to run alongside gifted and talented summer schools already provided by local authorities and individual schools.

- Secondary schools will be encouraged to make greater use of **grouping by ability** in order to meet the needs of the most able and to use **curriculum flexibility** to allow pupils to take Key Stage 3 tests and GCSE courses early and to mix academic and vocational courses.

- **At advanced level, a new extended project** will allow the most able students to demonstrate high scholastic ability.

- **Extended schools** (see later section).

- **More personalised learning** (see later section).

More information on *Higher Standards, Better Schools for All* can be found at www.dfes.gov.uk/publications/schoolswhitepaper.

Extended schools

In many parts of the country, extended schools are already operating, but it is intended that schools will become much more central in providing a wide range of services to children, parents and the community. The government intends to spend £680 million by 2008 to facilitate these developments. Ideally these services should include:

- all-year childcare from 8.00am to 6.00pm

- referral to a wide range of support services, such as speech therapy, mental health and behaviour support

- exciting activities, including study support and extension/enrichment activities that will motivate the most able

- parenting support, which might include classes on healthy eating, helping children with homework, dealing with challenging behaviour, etc.

- community use of school facilities, especially ICT.

Again, this is an initiative that will benefit all children, especially those whose carers work. However, there are particular benefits for those children whose school performance suffers because they have nowhere to study at home and for those with talents that parents cannot nurture because of limited means.

More information on extended schools can be found at www.teachernet. gov.uk/settingup and www.tda.gov.uk/remodelling/extendedschools.aspx.

Personalised learning

As mentioned earlier in this chapter, a key component of current education reforms is the emphasis on personalised learning – maximising potential by tailoring education to individual needs, strengths and interests. The key features of personalised learning are:

- **Assessment for Learning** – Information from data and the tasks and assessments pupils undertake must be used to feed back suggestions about how work could be improved and what learning they need to do next. But the feedback should be a two-way process with pupils also providing information to teachers about factors impeding their learning and approaches that would enhance it. This feedback should inform future lesson planning. For the most able pupils, effective assessment for learning should mean that they move forward with their learning at an appropriate pace and depth, rather than marking time while others catch up.

- **Effective Teaching and Learning Strategies** – It is still the case that many teachers teach only in the way that was most successful for them as learners. There is ample evidence that our most able pupils do not form an homogeneous group and that, in order to bring out their many and varied gifts and talents, we need to adopt a wide range of teaching strategies, making full use of the opportunities provided by ICT. At the same time pupils need to become aware of the learning strategies that are most successful for them, whilst also exploring a broader range of learning approaches.

- **Curriculum Entitlement and Choice** – There are many examples of highly gifted adults whose abilities were masked at school because the curriculum did not appear to be relevant to them. Schools need to take the opportunities afforded by new flexibility in the curriculum, by the specialised diplomas of study being introduced for 14- to 19-year-olds and by partnership with other schools, colleges and businesses to engage their pupils. There are several schools now where more able pupils cover Key Stage 3 in two years. The year that is freed up by this approach can be used in a variety of ways, such as starting GCSE courses early, following an enrichment programme or taking up additional science and language courses. The possibilities are endless if there is desire for change.

- **School Organisation** – Effective personalisation demands a more flexible approach to school organisation. This flexibility might show itself in the way teaching and support staff are deployed, by the way pupils are grouped, by the structure of the school day and by the way in which ICT is used to enable learning to take place beyond the classroom. At least one school is abandoning grouping by age in favour of grouping by ability in the hope that this will provide the necessary challenge for the most able. It remains to be seen how successful this approach is but experimentation and risk-taking is essential if we are to make schooling relevant and exciting for our most able pupils.

- **Partnerships Beyond Schools** – Schools cannot provide adequately for their most able pupils without making full use of the opportunities and expertise offered by other groups within the community, including parents together with family support groups, social and health services, sports clubs and other recreational and business organisations.

The websites www.standards.dfes.gov.uk/personalisedlearning and www.teachernet. gov.uk/publications/ will provide more information on personalised learning, whilst new curriculum opportunities to be offered to 14- to 19-year-olds are described in www.dfes.gov.uk/14-19.

Self-evaluation and inspection

The most able must have as many opportunities for development as other pupils. Poor, unchallenging teaching or an ideology that confuses equality of opportunity with levelling down should not hinder their progress. They should have a fair share of a school's resources both in terms of learning materials and in human resources. The environment for learning should be one in which it is safe to be clever and to excel. These are points that schools should consider when preparing their self-evaluation and school development plans.

There have been dramatic changes in the relationships between schools and local authorities and in the schools' inspection regime since the Children Act 2004. Local authorities are now regarded as commissioners for services for children. One of their tasks is to facilitate the appointment of SIPs, School Improvement Partners, who act as the main conduit between schools and LAs and take part in an 'annual conversation' with their schools when the school's self-evaluation and progress towards targets is discussed.

Self-evaluation is also the cornerstone of the new shorter, more frequent Ofsted inspections, using a SEF (self-evaluation form) as a central point of reference together with the five outcomes for children of *Every Child Matters*. An invaluable tool for schools recognising that they need to do more for their gifted and talented pupils, or simply wanting to assess their current provision, is the institutional quality standards for gifted and talented education (IQS).

Institutional quality standards for gifted and talented education (IQS)

These standards, developed by a partnership of the DfES, NAGTY and other interested groups, are an essential self-evaluation tool for any school focusing on its gifted and talented provision. Under each of five headings, schools look carefully at the level indicators and decide which of the three levels they have achieved:

- **Entry level** – a school making its first steps towards developing a whole-school policy might find that much of its provision falls into this category. Ofsted would rate such provision satisfactory.

- **Developing level** – where there is some effective practice but there is room for development and improvement. This aligns with a good from Ofsted.

- **Exemplary level** – where good practice is exceptional and sustained. Ofsted would rate this excellent.

The five headings show clear links to the personalisation agenda: effective teaching and learning strategies; enabling curriculum entitlement and choice; assessment for learning; school organisation; and strong partnerships beyond school.

Having identified the levels at which they are performing, schools are then able to draw up development plans. A copy of these standards is included in the appendices and more information about them can be found at www2.teachernet. gov.uk/qualitystandards.

Resources for teachers and parents of more able pupils

There is currently an abundance of resources and support agencies for teachers, parents and gifted and talented young people themselves. A few of general interest are included below. Other history examples will be found in later chapters of this book.

World Class Tests

These have been introduced by QCA to allow schools to judge the performance of their most able pupils against national and international standards. Currently tests are available for 9- and 13-year-olds in mathematics and problem solving. Some schools have found that the problem solving tests are effective at identifying able underachievers in maths and science. The website contains sample questions so that teachers, parents and pupils themselves can assess the tests' suitability for particular pupils or groups of pupils, and the tests themselves are also available online. For more information go to www. worldclassarena.org.uk.

National Curriculum Online

This website, administered by QCA, provides general guidance on all aspects of the National Curriculum but also has a substantial section on general and subject-specific issues relating to gifted and talented education, including identification strategies, case studies, management and units of work. Details of the National Curriculum Online can be found at www.nc.uk.net/gt.

G&TWise

G&TWise links to recommended resources for gifted and talented pupils, checked by professionally qualified subject editors, in all subjects and at all key stages and provides up-to-date information for teachers on gifted and talented education. Details can be found at www2.teachernet.gov.uk.

NACE – the National Association for Able Children in Education

NACE is an independent organisation that offers support for teachers and other professionals trying to develop provision for gifted and talented pupils. It gives advice and guidance to teachers and others, runs courses and conferences, provides consultants and keynote speakers.

It has also produced the NACE Challenge Award Framework, which it recommends could be used alongside IQS, as it exemplifies evidence and action planning. While IQS indicates what needs to be improved, the Challenge Award Framework suggests how to effect change. More information can be found at www.nace.co.uk.

National Association for Gifted Children (NAGC)

NAGC is a charity providing support for gifted and talented children and young people and their parents and teachers. It has a regional structure and in some parts of the country there are branch activities for children and parents. NAGC provides: counselling for both young people and their parents; INSET and courses for teachers; publications; activities for 3- to 10-year-olds; and a dedicated area (to which they have exclusive access) on their website for 11- to 19-year-olds, called Youth Agency. For further information go to www. nagcbritain.org.uk.

Children of High Intelligence (CHI)

CHI acts on behalf of children whose intelligence puts them above the 98th percentile. It often acts in a support capacity when parents are negotiating appropriate provision with schools and local authorities. For further details visit www.chi-charity.org.uk.

Summary

- Schools must provide suitable challenge and support for their most able pupils.
- Appropriate provision can enhance motivation and improve behaviour.
- Recent legislation to support disadvantaged children should mean that fewer potentially gifted and talented children fall through the net.
- Effective self-evaluation of school provision for gifted and talented pupils and challenging targets are the keys to progress.
- There are many agencies that can help teachers with this work.

CHAPTER 2

Departmental policy and approach

- The role of the subject leader
- The departmental gifted and talented coordinator
- Departmental policy
- Organisational issues
- INSET activities

Introduction

School life is classroom life. The quality of experiences that an able child in history will enjoy will be determined by individual classroom teachers. However, what those individual teachers do in the classroom; what they determine to be important; their understanding of what is the best way of supporting able children and impacting on their learning is influenced by the departmental context. The role of the subject leader is, with the exception of what happens in their own classroom, in many ways an indirect role. Subject leaders must promote an environment that allows the people they are leading to function at their best and to develop a clear understanding of what will work within their own classrooms.

However, the chapter begins with an explanation as to why the history department might want to focus on its more able pupils.

An argument for focusing on the able child can be based around the ideas of inclusion and challenge.

Inclusion

The 'able' have been defined by the DfES as the top ten per cent of a given school population. This is a sizeable proportion of pupils whose needs are to be addressed. A clear argument in this book is that these pupils do have specific needs that cannot be met simply by asking them to fulfil the content requirements of a scheme of work or syllabus. External accountability measures draw our attention to pupils who are on the C/D borderline and those who need support to access grades F–G. This is because these are the two measures that are used on public league tables. This is understandable, but there is an entitlement issue for those who are capable of or likely to achieve far more.

Challenge

The second point is that concentrating on the F–G or C–D boundaries may decrease levels of challenge and achievement in lessons.

Focusing on the work of the most able pupils involves an examination of what good and challenging history work looks like. It helps staff concentrate on the thinking that is required for excellent performance. It helps define what we want the best in our pupils to be. It helps create dialogue between a model of excellence, the needs of our pupils and the materials, strategies and tools we can use to move those pupils on. Although the original focus might be on the top ten per cent of the ability range, teachers will find that the number of pupils who can access these resources, in some form, is considerably higher. By expanding their understanding of what intelligence is, as described in Chapter 3, and by making challenging tasks more accessible, as described in Chapter 4, teachers will identify more pupils as being able in history, and be able to provide appropriately challenging and engaging work.

The role of the subject leader – leading and learning

Before we examine the subject leader standards in detail we are going to examine two general approaches to departmental development.

Building capacity versus compliance

Building capacity
Louise Stoll (2003) defines capacity as the ability of an organisation to engage in sustainable change. The characteristics that make this kind of change sustainable include:

- a focus on what will make a difference rather than ephemera

- a focus on internal culture – the explicit construction of joint understandings and meanings, e.g. what does gifted and talented mean to us in the context of this particular school/department?

- ways of working which emphasise learning rather than compliance

- ways of working which emphasise collaboration rather than individual endeavour

- ways of working that distributes leadership – so that leadership becomes a function to which many contribute rather than a role held by a few.

The inability of schools to do this is well documented. A lot of 'change' that takes place in schools can be best characterised as surface or structural change, rather than change in culture, attitudes, dispositions and ways of working. It might include changes in organisation or changes in documentation. In other words an initial response to change is to re-examine a scheme of work or a policy. Schools are quite adept at producing evidence of change without actually changing what takes place in the classroom. This is important because what happens in the classroom is dominated more by culture and expectation and the thinking of individual teachers, than by formal policies which may be imposed upon them.

It is the classroom that counts. It is at classroom level that learning takes place. It is the point of contact between teacher and learner. The difficulty for subject leaders, and senior managers for that matter, is that with the exception of their own classrooms, they only have an indirect influence over classrooms of others. Arguably performance management has begun to redress this, but teachers can often teach to 'tick the boxes' for external bodies one day (SMT, Ofsted) and then revert to their normal mode of teaching the next.

This is not due to intransigence. The reason for a lack of change might be due to a number of reasons which may include the following.

Compliance versus learning culture

A compliance culture looks for conformity. It takes what constitutes 'good' as a given and monitors for its implementation. Teachers are often told that they have to do things because of outside accountability measures: Ofsted demands this or performance management demands that. Models have been constructed of 'good' or 'best' practice, which teachers are expected to replicate.

This process ignores the changes that those people went through originally to construct that notion of 'best practice': the development of new ideas and the rejection of old ones and misconceptions; the making of mistakes and learning by them; the discovery of which routes led to dead ends and which led to greener pastures. This process in itself means that the teachers have internalised the change they are trying to effect. It becomes a part of their **instinctive repertoire**. At this point it can be seen to have a dramatic effect on pupils. The expectation is that this practice can be disseminated to others who can replicate the practice themselves. This ignores the process that others have gone through; it ignores the relationship between this process and the impact on pupils. Replicated practice does not have the same impact on pupils as internalised use does. The result of this is that there is not enough time for teachers to reflect on the impact that changes in practice can have. They do not have enough opportunities to create a dialogue between the needs of their pupils and the strategies they have at their disposal.

A learning culture in a school brings the process of creating a dialogue between the needs of the pupils and the strategies teachers have at their disposal to the foreground. It recognises that teachers must have the time to reflect, practise, modify and change their ways of working. It recognises that such a process is, and has to be, continuous. This is because there is a dynamic between the changing demands and needs of pupils and the expanding, changing repertoire of the teacher that will only stop when children stay the same from one class and one year group to the next.

Time, structures and priorities

There is never enough time. What subject leaders need to be able to do better is to distinguish between what is important and what is urgent; what can be relegated to the end of agenda items so that there can be a focus on teaching and learning; how teachers can learn what is the best way to help **their** able pupils in **their** classrooms. It would be an understatement to say that this is not easy. However, we can look at the constraints around us and see how far we can wriggle out of them.

Self-awareness and expectations

Teaching can be a very lonely job. Although in most schools the days where the classroom door was closed and nobody entered are gone, it is still true that most teachers spend most of their time with their children by themselves. The opportunities therefore for staff to actually see what is going on in other classrooms is limited. This may seem a little perverse as teachers spend a good deal of their time observing children, intervening with them and teaching them. However, this view lacks perspective and time for reflection. A teacher is just too busy in the classroom. This problem is compounded by the fact that when teachers are given an opportunity of feedback on their teaching, the dialogue that takes place is one between the teaching that was observed and predetermined teaching models that are judged to be good, satisfactory or excellent, etc. This is not the same as teachers analysing their own teaching, thinking about the **consequences** of their teaching on pupil learning and considering the potential impact of changes of their pedagogy on pupil learning. It is the difference between a summative evaluation of a lesson and a coaching conversation between colleagues about the learning in a classroom.

A successful head of department might find that owing to these pressures their colleagues articulate a number of beliefs:

- We don't need to look at the gifted and talented because they'll do all right anyway.

- We have to look at gifted and talented because it is an expectation of us – we are in an Excellence Cluster.

- All this means is that we have to compile a register and complete the paperwork.

- Teaching able children is no different to teaching any other children – we just have to provide the occasional extension task on the worksheet.

- Able children are just those children who can do the work that we set them correctly.

- Able children are those children who can write a little bit more.

To tackle these misconceptions a successful subject leader will lead their department in ways that:

- create awareness of how supporting the able will positively impact on others

- allow teachers to think and reflect upon why they might want to focus on the able children in the school – how might it benefit them – how might it benefit everybody else

- create self-awareness amongst teachers of the practices they do already

- work in a collaborative way with colleagues to explore new pedagogical approaches and draw up new policies

- maximise departmental time for learning – find other ways to deal with administrative matters

- encourage teachers to take risks with their teaching and learning.

Some successful heads of department have found the following strategies useful:

- Discussing and evaluating lesson plans and materials. It helps tremendously if the head of department takes risks as well. The head of department could present materials from a lesson at a departmental meeting and give the staff two or three discussion points. It is even better if the head of department presents a lesson which is satisfactory rather than exemplary – a mixture of good points with room for improvement.

- Discussing and evaluating a video-taped lesson. It is best to ask your line manager on the SMT for permission to do this because the protocols and procedures on video-taping children are changing and there should be a school policy for you to conform to. However, if this is possible it is invaluable as it helps create that all-important self-awareness. It also helps a wider audience view a lesson developing. Needless to say all the previous comments about the head of department leading hold true here more than at any other time.

- Peer coaching. Space precludes a full description of how a peer-coaching programme might be carried out. However, a sense of peer coaching might be obtained if we view it as professional dialogue between equals. It is a way of conducting lesson observations with a focus on pupil learning rather than teacher performance. See Appendix 2.1 to this chapter and later references.

- Collaborative planning. This is an extremely profitable way of building the capacity of the department and getting people to focus on learning. Start by taking a sequence of lessons from a scheme of work. Then ask the department to consider what they want the children to learn in each lesson (the learning objectives). You may find that the department is surprised by how they articulate this. They may find that they need to work quite hard to articulate with precision what it is they want pupils to learn rather than do or the content they will cover. There may be a tendency to articulate the learning in terms of knowledge rather than understanding and skills as well. Discussion may provoke colleagues to think about what aspects of learning are explicit with children and what aspects might remain implicit. Secondly, discuss with the department how you would expect pupils to demonstrate that learning – it might be what they have produced, a process they have demonstrated or what they have said. Then ask them to differentiate them. What would they expect **all**, **most** and **some** to achieve? Then ask them whether they think the **some** outcomes are realistic outcomes for their able children.

- Produce a departmental bulletin of useful materials and ideas. If the department is large, i.e. part of a humanities faculty, then it might be worthwhile making this a formal newsletter. On the other hand it might be more convenient simply to have a pin board in the departmental office area so that people can attach suggestions and tips of what works. (This has been done successfully in a number of schools.)

- Produce a departmental booklet. This is more than a policy statement, but the booklet could include it. Collaboratively ask the department to think through and produce a set of methods for identification, a set of key learning outcomes for the able in each year group, and more importantly a selection of activities, questions, approaches and topics that they think work particularly well. The aim of this is to make the department think hard about what they want to do and produce something to formalise that thinking rather than simply produce a glossy piece of paper that looks nice. This book contains enough ideas to be useful as a starting point.

The subject leader and leadership standards

The subject leader who begins working with their department in this manner will be achieving a number of the standards for subject leaders as set by the Teacher Development Agency. The principal ones include:

> Core Purpose: To provide professional leadership and management for a subject to secure high quality teaching, effective use of resources and improved standards of learning and achievement for all pupils.

A subject leader who is using some or all of these capacity building tools will certainly be providing professional leadership. The department will be working through and building a shared understanding and vision of what high quality teaching looks like. A focus on the able will improve their outcomes and achievements and by providing access to these materials for a wider audience should result in better outcomes for entire cohorts.

> A subject leader plays a key role in supporting, guiding and motivating teachers of the subject, and other adults. Subject leaders evaluate the effectiveness of teaching and learning, the subject curriculum and progress towards targets for pupils and staff, to inform future priorities and targets for the subject.

By using capacity building strategies the successful subject leader will be supporting, guiding and motivating colleagues. By using these strategies and engaging in dialogue over a particular group of pupils then evaluation of the appropriateness of the curriculum and resources, etc. is being done as well.

Outcomes
a. pupils who

show sustained improvement in their subject knowledge, understanding and skills in relation to prior attainment; understand the key ideas in the subject at a level appropriate to their age and stage of development; show improvement in their literacy, numeracy and information technology skills; know the purpose and sequence of activities; are well prepared for any tests and examinations in the subject; are enthusiastic about the subject and highly motivated to continue with their studies; through their attitudes and behaviour, contribute to the maintenance of a purposeful working environment.

This is what we want to achieve for our able pupils. A focus on the able can help raise standards amongst the rest of the cohort as teachers naturally will want to provide the widest audiences amongst their pupils to access materials for the able.

b. teachers who

work well together as a team; support the aims of the subject and understand how they relate to the school's aims; are involved in the formation of policies and plans and apply them consistently in the classroom; are dedicated to improving standards of teaching and learning; have an enthusiasm for the subject which reinforces the motivation of pupils; have high expectations for pupils and set realistic but challenging targets based on a good knowledge of their pupils and the progression of concepts in the subject; make good use of guidance, training and support to enhance their knowledge and understanding of the subject and to develop expertise in their teaching; take account of relevant research and inspection findings; make effective use of subject-specific resources; select appropriate teaching and learning approaches to meet subject-specific learning objectives and the needs of pupils.

By using capacity building strategies the department will be working closely as a team and will be jointly formulating policies and applying them consistently in the classroom. Working through the materials in this book can help teachers formulate high expectations and help develop expertise in their teaching. This book is also designed to help provide INSET activities and highlight CPD opportunities.

The departmental gifted and talented coordinator

It has been argued that if a department is to make the most of this opportunity then a collaborative approach is necessary. The way of working for the department may be that of action research, but at the end of the day somebody has to take responsibility for making things happen. The first point to emphasise is that this is not necessarily the subject leader. It may be part of somebody else's professional development to take on this role. This is a capacity building tool in itself.

Devon LA specifies a number of tasks for the gifted and talented coordinator.

Role of gifted and talented coordinator (Devon LA)

- Identify gifted and talented pupils; *this is to include the upkeep of a register of gifted and talented pupils working within the department; to identify and select the best identification tools that can be used – both generic and subject specific; to be responsible for drawing up a departmental definition of what an able pupil in history might look like in their school.*

- Increase teacher awareness of the needs of these pupils; *lead appropriate INSET within the department.*

- Enable teachers to adapt and adjust to the academic and social needs of gifted and talented pupils; *provide expertise within the department to support other teachers' repertoire of approaches for the more able and strategies to foster a climate for learning.*

- Ensure that all teachers are able to share in providing the level of subject support needed; *identify historical resources that can be used and disseminate them within the department; highlight those opportunities in Schemes of Work.*

- Draw on a range of sources of support for these pupils; *specifically – to be responsible for liaison with different departments – particularly within the humanities area – the local university – the local branch of the Historical Association – SEN department – library and museum service – school library.*

- Review the progress of each individual; *be responsible for regular monitoring and assessment of able pupils and tracking their achievement.*

Departmental policy

The clear principle of establishing a successful departmental policy is that it should reflect the work that the department does and its aspirations rather than be a model of what should be that is never subsequently referred to – there should be a sense of ownership amongst the department.

What to include in a more able or gifted and talented subject policy

The subject policy should follow the same framework as the school policy and fit in with its general philosophy. A good policy will develop from:

- a thorough and honest audit of existing levels of achievement of the most able and of their attitudes to learning

- clear identification of where changes need to be made and the drawing-up of an action plan

- consultation with senior management, G&T coordinator, other staff in the department and pupils

- the existence of effective strategies to monitor and evaluate the measures taken.

The following headings might be used when preparing a departmental or subject policy (words in italics are suggestions for subject-specific content or modifications):

Policy rationale and aims

- How does the policy relate to the school's overall aims and values? *Specifically refer here to the school aims and objectives and show how the objectives of this policy specifically relate to them.*

- How does the subject contribute to the young person's academic and personal development? *History's contribution to pupil learning and development might include some or all of the following: building up a series of frames of reference about the past that help inform pupils' understandings of the present and that enlarge pupils' understandings of what it means to be human; develop critical thinking skills with particular reference to explanations and the use of source material as evidence; develop pupils' literacy skills; place current institutions in their historical context and allow pupils to explore historical situations that contribute to their education for citizenship.*

- What does the department aim to provide for the most able students? *It is easy at this point to make a generalised aspirational statement about expected outcomes or state that able pupils are entitled to high quality teaching and learning. What is more effective is to describe how the experiences of the able will differ – with appropriate examples. Will you specify that there are different expected learning outcomes for the more able? Will there be more opportunities for them to evaluate source material, or interpretations in class? Will there be opportunities for them to pursue individual projects in class time – perhaps to examine some non-mainstream historical topics? Will they have opportunities to trace developments and changes over a longer period of time? If the answer to these questions is yes – where are you going to do it?*

Definitions

- In the context of your school and subject what do you mean by most able or gifted and/or talented? *This needs careful consideration. You can define the most able by a general statement – i.e. the top 10 per cent of ability in the school – but you also need to define them in terms of the potential ability of pupils and the specific historical knowledge, attributes, skills and dispositions you want to see. Use the subject specific checklist in Appendix 3.2.*

Identification

- How does your department's approach fit in with the school's practice on identification? *The departmental approach will build upon and incorporate the school policy. Therefore if there is a school reliance on predictive data then you will have to conform to it.*

- What subject-specific identification strategies will you use? *Will there be the use of departmental assessments that focus on specific key elements; how can you check for attitudes and dispositions to the subject?*

Organisational issues

- How will teaching groups be organised to meet the needs of all pupils including the most able? *A clear decision has to be made about whether the pupils will be placed in sets. There is still a tendency for history groups to be mixed ability, especially at Key Stage 4. However, if this is the case then teachers need to specify how able children will reach higher learning outcomes and show this in their planning.*

- Will fast tracking, early entry or acceleration to an older age group be considered and what measure will be taken to support these pupils and to ensure that they continue to make progress? *Here an explicit statement needs to be made. It is unlikely that pupils will be accelerated through Key Stage 3 – but there are going to be increasing options available at Key Stages 4 and 5 post-Tomlinson.*

Provision in lessons

- How do schemes of work and lesson plans reflect the demands to be made of the most able students? *This will mainly be through learning outcomes. You will specify the learning outcomes for the most able in individual lessons. You will specify yearly outcomes for the more able on longer term plans. Where there are opportunities for the more able to deviate from expected routes then this needs to be specified as well.*

- How will the need for faster pace, more breadth and greater depth in the subject be met? *An important point here is that if we expect higher outcomes from our more able pupils then they might not need to achieve the lower outcomes for the less able children. Breadth – in the plenary session how often are pupils asked to make connections from what they have learnt in this lesson to what they have learnt in previous lessons and in other units? Depth – this is going to be more than allowing them extra material. It might be giving them extra opportunities through homework to investigate topics in depth, or by providing different opportunities in lesson time. It might be that they do get access to different materials – more complex sources for example.*

- How are the thinking skills needed for this subject to be developed? *Here we need to be very careful for as history teachers, we will be delivering on two types of thinking skill. We will be contributing to cross-curricular thinking skills that are identified in the National Curriculum, e.g. pupil reasoning, information processing, creativity, etc. There is also the requirement to develop pupils' historical thinking as defined by the key elements and the GCSE criteria. This needs to be systematically planned.*

- How will different learning styles of pupils be catered for? *There might be opportunities to allow pupils to choose the product of the lesson, i.e. for some pupils to produce a mind map, an explanatory piece of writing or a kinaesthetic model. The teacher should, over a sequence of lessons, plan for a variety of learning styles to be used.*

- How will homework and independent learning be used to enhance their education? *Do not simply state that homework is seen to be a way of supporting pupil learning. It might be that simply asking pupils to repeat the skills that they have used in class is futile. However, the chance to build upon independent learning is good. If this is the approach that the department will take then what independent learning skills will be explicitly taught through homework and when will this occur?*

- How is assessment, both formative and summative, used to enable suitable targets to be set and appropriate progress to be made? *There will be an issue here of compliance with the school assessment policy. This will usually stipulate the frequency of summative assessments that are to be made on each pupil. These are likely to range from once every half term to once per year to once per Key Stage. It is likely that pupils will negotiate a numerical target. The formative assessment that takes place in the classroom is to enable pupils to reflect upon their progress in their learning. For it to be meaningful this reflection has to be about a concrete piece of learning, e.g. a specific learning objective or specific piece of work. Reflections on level descriptors, even if they are in pupil speak, tend to be generalised statements and actions rather than the specifics of learning. Assessment for learning is a crucial tool for the able as well as all other pupils.*

Out-of-class activities

- Activities beyond the classroom – *what trips will pupils go on and how will they extend pupil learning; what is the role of the school history club?*

- Study support for the most able – *do able pupils have older pupils as learning mentors; are they able to have tutorials with members of staff over crucial pieces of work?*

- Collaboration with outside agencies – *what links will able pupils have with the Historical Association, the local university or archaeological society?*

Transfer and transition

- How are students, who move on to sixth forms in other schools or colleges, supported? *What choice does the department offer post-16 if appropriate; does the department offer the advanced extension award; what guidance is given to pupils who want to study history at undergraduate level?*

Resources

- How are teaching assistants, learning mentors and other adult helpers used to support the most able?

- What outside agencies are used?

- What specific learning resources are available for the most able? *Moving beyond the textbook – historical fiction, accessible non-fiction sources, computer programs, TV material and the internet.*

Monitoring and evaluation

- Who is responsible for liaising with the school coordinator and developing good practice for the most able in your department? *Will it be the head of department or another nominated member?*

- How is the effectiveness of this policy to be measured? *This is actually two questions: the first being what criteria will be used to determine the success of this policy; the second what tools will be used to assess the impact of the policy. It is easy to build in numerical targets – the proportion of pupils who achieve high grades, go on to study history post-16 and at university – what is more difficult is to draw up success criteria for more qualitative targets. How are we to judge the quality of experience for pupils in classrooms?*

- What targets does the department have for its most able students (e.g. Levels 7 and 8 at Key Stage 3, A* and A at GCSE)? *More importantly how are those targets generated; how are they shared with pupils and how is progress towards them tracked?*

- How and when is the progress of individual students and groups monitored?

- What CPD is needed or will be provided? *This is an ongoing issue. Departments will not have a checklist of what must be covered but an ongoing dialogue between the needs of their pupils and their professional skills. CPD covers a range of methods, one of which is the INSET course – more profitable CPD will be classroom based, e.g. coaching.*

Auditing current provision

Establishing a policy is one issue; determining action is another. A department will need to focus its actions if these are to make an impact.

Many schools will have used the subject audit that accompanies the Key Stage 3 National Strategy. The audit included as Appendix 2.2 uses some of the strategies included in that document as well as others that relate directly to provision for the most able.

The first part of this audit is simple. It will be very familiar to anybody who has engaged in whole-school review processes before. It tries to identify who your able pupils are by attainment. The use of data can still be unfamiliar to heads of department and a good resource to refer to is the *Numbers Game: Using Assessment Data in Schools* by Keith Hedger and David Jesson (1998). This might give you a guideline to what your more able pupils are achieving at the moment and their attainment and achievement compared to national averages.

Identifying areas for development is more problematic. The departmental coordinator might want to consider some of the following issues:

- What actions are likely to have the largest impact on pupils as they are in the classroom? *A history club may be a good eventual outcome but is it the same as impacting on pupil experiences on a regular weekly basis?*

- Are there some areas which need to be addressed even though they will only have an indirect effect? *Lesson structure and the use of objectives might not have the immediate impact on pupils that we might want, but what else might it allow us to do, and what might its neglect prevent us from doing?*

- What is the scale and scope of our action? *Will all classes and year groups be tackled at the same time or will the department experiment with a few classes first, determine the teacher learning and then move outwards?*

- Success criteria: these are best expressed as pupil outcomes rather than changes in teaching or whether certain things are present. *Instead of saying that objectives will be communicated to the pupils say that pupils, when asked, will be able to distinguish what they are learning from what they are doing and ideally explain the relationship between the two.*

- How to monitor progress. *This is difficult and it is a little bit more than just determining whether the success criteria have been achieved. These things are very rarely 'tickable' if they are to be more than superficial. (SMART is rarely smart.) You might want to think about what change you might see, after five minutes, in a lesson, after a month, after a term or a year. If there is an issue with a slow rate of progress then does it mean that the action you are following is inappropriate and needs to be changed? If you are constructing a line of enquiry rather than a rigid plan then flexibility is more of a key rather than whether initial objectives were achieved.*

- Resources: these come in all sorts of shapes and sizes – time, money and materials. *Will you need money for supply cover to enable a coaching programme or series of lesson observations to take place? Is there the need for an outside consultant; to be 'gifted' time to enable people to go on the internet to cull sources for a particular enquiry or to construct open learning material? Resources can mean more than books or an electronic whiteboard.*

In short the departmental coordinator is being asked to construct a line of enquiry, to determine what the needs of the department's more able pupils are, to consider and implement necessary actions and to adapt those actions as staff monitor progress and refine their understanding of pupil needs.

Organisational issues

Alternative acceleration and enrichment models

Traditionally history departments have not provided an accelerated learning model for their students. It is still more common to find that GCSE groups are taught in mixed ability classes rather than grouped sets. At Key Stage 3 it is more common to find departments following a school policy. In other words if the school sets at Key Stage 3 then the department will, but if there is no requirement to do so then it is unlikely that the department will elect for it. The main point is that under either system it is necessary to plan for pupil learning via objectives and specified outcomes. It is clear from Chapter 4 that able pupils will need to have higher outcomes planned for them than others.

The 14–19 Education White Paper will allow pupils to study a mix of vocational and academic learning in the form of diplomas. There is also the possibility of pupils studying for the International Baccalaureate or even Open University modules early. It is possible to see the development of vocational learning as a threat to the position of history in the curriculum. However, it is also possible that these developments will help pupils to see the relevance of history and apply their skills in different contexts. A case study of how this might work is exemplified by the hybrid GCSE for history being prepared by QCA:

> The aim of this project is to develop a new GCSE that links history to related vocational areas of learning such as heritage, museums, galleries, sites, archaeology, tourism, media and law. It also offers a unique opportunity to trial new approaches to teaching, learning and assessment in history at GCSE, building on the existing good practice increasingly seen in many schools, especially at Key Stage 3. Students could, for example, be assessed on their ability to design and write a series of web pages for a local historical site, or to critically evaluate an existing museum display depicting a period of history they have studied during the course.
>
> (QCA *Winter Update* 2004)

The structure of the course has a lot of potential. Pupils will follow a core content unit. It is possible to spread that unit over either one or two years. That might mean that able pupils could study a discrete area in one year and then spend the second year working to a full GCSE. Then pupils will study two further modules each worth 25 per cent of the overall marks. The modules are to be selected from a menu of vocational and applied studies. Perhaps instead of the hybrid GCSE a useful title might be history and heritage studies. At one point it was mooted that if pupils were able to take sufficient modules then they could qualify for a double award.

The movement away from very focused and closed assessment tasks is to be welcomed. If the key characteristics of able pupils are things like creativity, independence and the ability to research then this allows these talents to be exploited and developed. What is more intriguing is that it is possible that the mark scheme for the units will not only specify the pupil outcomes, but also the level of support from the teacher. In other words to get an A* pupils will have to have a good historical knowledge, good skills and be able to deploy them independently of teacher support. The requirement to apply historical knowledge, skills and understanding to real world situations will not only benefit the more able but weaker pupils as well.

Possible themes in the hybrid optional modules include: heritage management; heritage management: a comparative approach in the local setting; myth and marketing; an archaeological investigation; a development study in the changing role of a particular group in society; an ICT unit. This certainly broadens out the study from Nazi Germany.

Resource allocation

It is important that the more able get their fair share of departmental resources. 'Resource' needs to be defined broadly. It might be in terms of books and classroom material that will stretch them. It might be time with the teacher, other tutor or teaching assistant. Whatever resources are needed, the more able have a claim to their equitable distribution the same as everybody else. As far as written resources are concerned, there has been a tendency to buy for the middle of the ability range and supplement with re-enforcement materials for those with SEN. Resources for the most able have often been neglected.

Liaison with other departments

This is profitable on a number of levels:

- A central store of information held by a school coordinator can help monitor the progress of pupils globally and enable the provision between departments to be monitored.

- Sharing of lists of able pupils with comparable departments, e.g. English or Geography, can determine whether there is agreement and can help determine whether some pupils have 'slipped' through the net.

- Sharing of ideas between colleagues can generate further ideas – geography teachers might have expertise in thinking skills, history teachers expertise in literacy and related issues – can the departments learn from each other?

- Sharing of planning is particularly powerful. Two colleagues from different departments planning together a single lesson, or reciprocal lessons, is very useful. It allows the collaboration between them to focus on the pedagogy rather than getting bogged down in subject content and issues. A further challenge might be for two colleagues to plan together, but to actually deliver the lesson in the other person's subject area, e.g. a historian deliver a jointly planned English lesson and the English specialist the history lesson.

Learning diaries

A learning diary is a way for pupils to reflect upon the extent and nature of their learning. It provides a way for pupils to record their metacognitive activities. As it is a semi-formal document it allows a basis for monitoring some of the more intangible qualities that we still regard as important.

A learning diary is a journal that allows pupils to reflect on a daily or weekly basis. It might ask pupils to consider some, or all, of the following questions:

- What have you learnt this week?

- What steps did you do to acquire this learning?

- What things particularly helped you/hindered you?

- How have you progressed in key historical skills (e.g. cause and consequence, similarity and differences, connections between different aspects of the past, use of historical evidence, enquiry and interpretations)?

- What have you learnt about the past this week that you did not learn in lesson time?

Pupil responses to these types of question can be monitored. It would be inappropriate to ask pupils to hand these diaries in as they can be quite intimate or private. However, they could be used by pupils in the plenary and then the teacher could ask pupils about their responses, or they could be the basis of a 'tutorial conversation' between pupil and subject teacher/form tutor.

INSET activities

The following strategies may be useful to hard-pressed departmental coordinators who seek to develop their colleagues' learning regarding the teaching of the able.

- Take the National Curriculum attainment target for Level 7 and Level 8 (or whatever level is appropriate for your school). Break the target down into its key statements. Consider what an outcome would be in a classroom for each of the statements. For example, what does 'making connection between and across content and period' look like in a classroom?

- Take a large sheet of sugar paper and ask staff members to mentally reflect upon a couple of pupils who they would consider to be able. Then ask them to brainstorm the attributes that pupils should have to be able.

- Photocopy some pieces of able pupils' work (preferably onto A3) and ask staff to read and annotate the work with Post-it notes. The annotations should represent key features of the pupils' work – ideas they have produced, language they have used, levels of historical knowledge, insights gained, lack of misconceptions etc. Then ask staff to collate these annotations – can they be used to build up a sense of expectation of the more able, especially when compared to the work in the previous activities?

- Ask staff to consider the kinds of things that teachers do that makes work more challenging for pupils and the kinds of things that teachers do that merely makes things more difficult for them. Then after drawing out those ideas select five activities from books such as *Thinking Through History* by Peter Fisher (2002), *Enlivening Secondary History* by Peter Davies, Derek Lynch and Rhys Davies (2003) and *The Teacher's Toolkit* by Paul Ginnis (2002). Ask them to consider which of these activities are the most challenging and why; and how they would crank up the level of challenge in the other activities.

- Ask staff to consider a couple of exemplary lesson plans – allow them to focus on the learning objectives and outcomes. Encourage them to rewrite the outcomes to allow the more able to demonstrate higher levels of learning.

- Ask staff to help construct a pupil questionnaire that helps the more able pupils reflect upon the effectiveness of their own learning.

Key points from the chapter

1. The role of the subject leader is to lead the department through a process of change.

2. Teachers will have to learn, collaboratively, how to bring about that change in the contexts of their own classroom.

3. The subject leader will have to allow thinking time and dissent and allow that dissent to play itself out.

4. The subject leader will have to show how a focus on the able pupil will reward the department and its work as a whole, rather than being done because of compliance.

CHAPTER 3

Recognising high ability and potential

- Identification of able pupils
- The identification process
- Models of intelligence
- Learning styles

Introduction

This is a chapter of contradiction. It is commonly assumed that if we are defining the able in a school as the top ten per cent of the ability range then these pupils should stand out and be glaringly obvious to us. However, there are a number of paradoxes that confront us which make this job harder:

1. The tighter we try to define the ways in which able pupils can be defined, the more unsatisfactory the definition becomes.

2. The more we try to widen the definition of able children, the more difficult it becomes to measure.

3. The more reliable the definition and description of able children becomes, the more children we find who – at least partially – match that description.

4. Intelligence is not a fixed quality. It is at least in part a cultural phenomenon and most teachers would be interested in defining the **potential** of pupils to improve and be able.

5. The term 'able child' is relative. It is expressed as a percentage of a cohort. The ability of a cohort will vary in a school over time and between schools.

6. Schools sometimes use unhelpful indicators as measures of ability.

7. Chapter 2 highlighted the point that the process of working through a curricular issue is at least as equally important as its product.

The first two points relate to the following fact: learning and learners are complex subjects. If we use measurable 'objective' tools such as CAT scores or feedback from closed exams and tests then we are taking an outcome approach. This approach, by itself, ignores the qualitative indicators such as an enquiring mind, joy of the subject and a disposition to learn. However, whilst these later qualities may be crucial they are impossible to measure **objectively** and **absolutely** consistently.

The third and fourth points emphasise that the notion of the able is not static but a dynamic. It is fine for pupils to drop in and out of the register depending upon time, subject and their interests. The fourth point is an indicator that the school's notion of how to determine the able will change. An examination of teacher written feedback in schools sometimes indicates that teachers still reward pupils for:

- details and length of answer

- neatness of work

- replication by the pupils of the answer that the teacher has told them

- being compliant.

These are almost like the default settings we have and unless we consciously work to a different set of criteria this is what we fall back to. It means that this is likely to be the default settings for identifying the able as well – high CAT score and the ability to remember and write well.

The fifth point emphasises that this chapter cannot provide a set of simple answers. The solutions to your problems are based in the school and the department.

What this chapter will do is **model a process** by which a department can produce a set of criteria to identify their able children. The department will need to determine which are the fixed points – the things they definitely need to do so that they can identify the able – and what are the variables – the bits that can be changed and adapted to fit the conditions of department and school. The aim is to achieve consistency in the department and synchronisation with the school policy, not replicate the national picture or replicate 'good practice'. Good luck!

A process for finding your most able

Step 1 – Determine the outcomes that you wish able pupils to achieve

This step is important because it enables a department to do the following:

- determine the expected achievements of the able

- provide a measure to determine who is achieving this level already, and help identify who has the potential to reach this level of achievement

- inform planning – by unpicking a level of achievement we can identify what knowledge, skills, conceptual understandings and dispositions the children need to develop and consequently backtrack what needs to be taught in lessons

- clarify teacher thinking – what are the precise requirements? What might be the difference between explaining and analysing? What bits of the achievement levels are catered for and which bits need rebalancing?

- establishing a dialogue between pupil perceptions of the required standards and the actual requirements – what misconceptions do they have – for example the difference between precision and detail?

The following should be considered as a worked example. It takes one attainment standard – the exceptional performance level at Key Stage 3. It shows what can be done if an outcome statement is broken down and how it can help planning, thinking and pupil achievement.

The exceptional performance level description in the National Curriculum attainment targets reads as follows:

> Pupils use their extensive and detailed factual knowledge and understanding of the history of Britain and the wider world to analyse relationships between a wide range of events, people, ideas and changes and between the features of different past societies and cultures. Their explanations and analyses of reasons for, and results of, events and changes are well substantiated and set in the wider historical context. They analyse links between events and developments that took place in different countries and in different periods. They make balanced judgements based on their understanding of the historical context about the value of different interpretations of historical events and developments. Drawing on their historical knowledge and understanding, they use sources of information critically, carry out historical enquiries, develop, maintain and support an argument and reach and sustain substantiated and balanced conclusions independently. They select, organise and deploy a wide range of relevant information to produce consistently well-structured narratives, descriptions and explanations, making appropriate use of dates and terms.
>
> (National Curriculum Attainment Target for History – Exceptional Performance Level)

We shall now break down the attainment target into its constituent parts, paying particular attention to its 'cognitive stems' that indicate the level of thinking required.

Extensive and detailed

In any National Curriculum level descriptor, for any subject, the first sentence is an indicator of the level of knowledge that pupils should be demonstrating. Pupils' knowledge is expected to be 'extensive' and 'detailed'. However, it should be remembered that we are not dealing with university students but pupils who, for the most part, will be 14 years of age. Therefore, we are dealing with 'extensive' and 'detailed' within this context.

Extensive indicates the range and scope pupils have with their historical knowledge. **Detail** indicates the depth of knowledge that they have. The implication of this is that pupils have a large framework of the past. They are able to have the perspective of 'grand vision'. They are able to sequence events and have an excellent grasp of chronology. They are able to determine **significance** and **turning points**. They are able to draw upon material from within a particular period and across historical periods.

Detail or precision?

Anecdotal evidence suggests that in lots of cases pupils do a mental sleight of hand when they are told to put more detail in their answer. Sometimes it is clear that they translate the word 'detail' to mean length or volume of work. They think that the teacher wants them to simply write more, perhaps put in more effort or sometimes simply to write more neatly. This is a clear misconception as the teacher wants the pupil to do something quite different!

When we say 'detail' do we mean 'precision'? Precision to a child is different to detail because it takes the focus away from the length of a piece of work to the language that is being used. Instead of imprecise generalities we might want pupils to:

- give dates – either by year, month or precise date depending upon the context of the piece of work

- give numerical information if describing trends

- use people's names

- use place names where appropriate

- use precise, appropriate, historical conventions and vocabulary.

It does not mean that simply by being more precise that a pupil is producing better historical work. We are not asking pupils to return to the days of O level when they had simply to regurgitate historical fact as uncritical information, but we are asking them to use historical knowledge as **historical punctuation**. In the same way as the use of grammar and punctuation can give meaning, shape and understanding to language and discourse, the use of historical knowledge gives shape, meaning and understanding to historical explanations and analyses. A page of writing with no punctuation is hard to decipher, a page of historical explanation that lacks precise content is equally hard to make sense of. Dates, events, names etc. provide a point of reference for the reader (or listener, or viewer depending upon the medium being used). It allows the pupil to pinpoint trends, cause and consequence, and place historical sources and interpretations into context.

A common misconception regarding 'extensive' is that it is seen as an aggregation of detail. How extensive something is is not cumulative, but it is about having a range of information. Consequently it is about understanding the significance of what you know. It is the difference between knowing the significance and importance of the Reformation and the 'icon' of Martin Luther nailing his 96 theses onto a church door in 1517, rather than knowing in detail everything that was in them. It is about being able to make connections between different content – for example, Martin Luther, the Reformation and the Dissolution of the Monasteries. Less able pupils treat historical knowledge as being at one level. This means they find it incredibly hard to discriminate between what they need to know and what it is safe to forget.

Analyse

The second part of the attainment target criteria says that pupils should be able to 'analyse a range of relationships in the past between people, events and ideas'. The cognitive stem for this sentence is **analyse**. It is a word that is frequently used by history teachers, who hold an implicit understanding of its meaning, but it is not always so clear to pupils.

To analyse something is to give a detailed examination of its structure. Therefore to be able to analyse pupils must:

- have a view of the whole of the phenomenon they are examining

- be able to break down that phenomenon into its constituent parts

- focus on the relationships between the constituent parts

- look at part–whole relationships

- reconstruct the initial subject after its parts have been re-examined.

This is quite a complex way of thinking. What students seem to be able to do better is to look at the constituent parts and explore some kind of linkage. What they find more challenging is actually deconstructing the subject into its constituent parts in the first place, and then reconstructing it at the end.

What is the difference between explaining and analysing?

Able pupils find it relatively easy to make the move from description to explanation, but their ability to make their explanations more analytical is more fraught. They need to be able to determine the difference between explaining and analysing. Within the context of the attainment target we might say that an explanation relies upon making events clear. It is to ascribe reasons, motives and events. In pupils' work we might expect to see causation working in a simple additive sense, e.g. A led to B, or A allowed B to happen, and that is probably how they will write, with one cause leading to another. If they are able to say which cause was the most important then it is likely that they will select one cause and assert its importance.

Analysis is more than cumulative thinking

An analysis will differ from explanation because the pupils will be thinking of the causes and features of an event in terms of their relationship with each other. They will think of causes as having a direct or indirect effect. They might be thinking of causes in terms of their necessity or sufficiency. Therefore, they might be thinking of those causes which create a background or general situation as well as specific triggers and be able to show the relationship between the two. This differs from linking the two sets of causes, which in many cases simply asserts that there is a link or demonstrates the link in a simple way.

Example

In 1939 the Second World War broke out in Europe. This was because Germany invaded Poland and both Britain and France had guaranteed Polish integrity of border. There are a number of reasons why war broke out including the Treaty of Versailles which Hitler had said he would destroy and Britain and France not wanting Germany to be too powerful. This is why they went to war. **Explanation**.

   The Second World War broke out in 1939 because there was a specific change in the policies of Britain and France towards Germany that Hitler did not recognise. The Treaty of Versailles had provided an agenda for German foreign policy since its inception and consequently Germany and the Western democracies were always interacting in this context. Whilst this was not enough to cause war it did mean that when an aggressively nationalist dictator took over Germany then war became more likely. **Analysis**.

The first example ascribes reasons while the second focuses on the relationships between them. This is the fundamental difference between explanation and analysis in causation.

   It is not only explanations that pupils will be analysing, but the relationship between ideas.

Examples

The ideas of William Harvey and the scientific revolution in seventeenth century England, or Robert Owen and Social Christianity in the nineteenth century.

Pupils can analyse the key features of past societies and make specific comparisons between them.

Analysing the key features of the Middle Ages, the feudal system, reliance upon agriculture, architecture, the nature of politics. An example of comparison might be the notion of Christendom and world views in the Middle Ages to those of nineteenth century Industrial Britain.

Not only should pupils identify the similarities and differences, they need to make judgements about why these similarities and differences exist. Is it because of changes in the economy; is it because of the voyages of discovery and the rise of humanism?

Analysing links between periods

The next part of the attainment target asks pupils to 'analyse links between events and developments that took place in different countries and in different periods'.

This is asking pupils to widen the scope of their studies and see links between different areas, for example: can they analyse the relationship and impact between the American and French revolutions, the so-called 'Atlantic Revolution'? Can they analyse the relationships between the British conquest of India from the seventeenth century to the 'Scramble for Africa' in the nineteenth?

The value of interpretation

They make a balanced judgement based on their understanding of the historical context about the value of different interpretations of historical events and developments.

Ofsted consistently reports that interpretations are taught weakly at Key Stage 3. An interpretation is a view of an historical event. It can be the interpretation of an historian or how the past has been represented. It is the focus on the contentious and controversial. It is the idea that the past has been written about and portrayed in different ways: audience and intent matter.

To determine a value of an interpretation pupils might need to do some or all of the following:

- Place the interpretation into an appropriate historical context. This is a little more than asking questions (normally who, what, when, where, why) about its provenance, rather asking how the interpretation was constructed.

- Sensitivity to audience and intent. Hayden White, writing in *Metahistory* (1974), may be wrong when he argues that historians shape their narrative to a predetermined plot outline, but interpretations, over time, do show sensitivity to the expectations of the audience.

- Intellectual consistency within the interpretation. This is asking pupils to think very hard about the interpretation – does it match their understanding of the event/concept? This is more than checking for the accuracy of the interpretation. It is about the weight and meaning that the historian has placed upon parts of their interpretation. It is about whether the conclusions drawn from the available evidence are valid. It is about whether the interpretation as a whole is reasonable.

Example

In Year 9, after studying the Munich Crisis and the debates concerning Appeasement, able pupils were asked to analyse an extract of *The Guilty Men* by Cato (1940). They were asked to place the source into a historical context and determine how valid the contemporary claims were about Chamberlain's failure over appeasement.

Critical sources

Drawing on their historical knowledge and understanding, they use sources of information critically, carry out historical enquiries, develop, maintain and support an argument and reach and sustain substantiated and balanced conclusions independently.

Use sources of information critically. This is more than a mechanical approach to the 'reliability' of a source. It is placing a source of information firmly within its historical context. It is thinking about the circumstances in which the source was produced. It is thinking about which questions we can legitimately ask of the source and which would be inappropriate – in other words using the source as part of a line of enquiry. There is also, of course, the question of how the source can be used beyond a piece of information but as evidence to support an argument. In what ways can it be used, how much weight can be put on it? There is the difference, as Marwick, writing in *The New Nature of History* (2001), pointed out, between its witting and unwitting testimony. Placing the source in a context allows the source to be evaluated critically. It will not be taken at face value but not approached mechanically either.

A balanced, substantiated conclusion means that pupils both justify rather than assert their conclusions and use precise terms to exemplify what they mean. **Balance** means that whilst they are able to put forward a conclusion they recognise the **extent of the validity** of their case. They will qualify it and recognise the exceptions and the limitations of their position.

Selection and relevance

They select, organise and deploy a wide range of relevant information to produce consistently well-structured narratives, descriptions and explanations, making appropriate use of dates and terms.

The key terms here are selection and relevance. This means that pupils do have a wide range of material at their disposal and they will select the most appropriate pieces of material that support their argument.

'Well-structured' means more than using paragraphs! If the form of communication is written then it means that there should be a logical order to the material that makes the argument the pupil is presenting explicit. There should not be a random order to the paragraphs but one which structures the argument.

Identification checklist

This process of unpicking a set of learning outcomes allows us to draw up the beginning of an identification checklist:

- Pupils use appropriate examples in their work – to illustrate a depth of understanding or to show understanding and links outside the immediate context of what they are studying.

- They show the interconnection and relationship between the events being studied.

- They can break down historical interpretations and think about the validity and reasonableness of such views.

- They can place historical sources and interpretations into a historical context – especially in describing how such material was produced or constructed.

- They can communicate their ideas fluently, not just in the written form, showing balance and a sound conclusion.

Step 2 – Specific history learner qualities

Having identified what kinds of outcomes we might want pupils to produce it is now useful to raise the sense of generality by one level. This next step looks for some of the harder-to-measure attributes that able pupils have, such as their attitude to the subject.

In an ideal world, pupils who are able in history will:

1. **be knowledgeable about the past**. They will be working with an expanding frame of reference. They will be making explicit links between what they are currently learning and what they have previously learnt. They will be making increasingly sophisticated analogies and seeing more subtle similarities and differences. Their frame of reference will span across and within a given historical period. It is also likely that they will 'specialise' in an area of the past and do some further reading and collect anecdotes and stories about the period or theme they are interested in.

2. **demonstrate an attitude and disposition to the past**. This sensitivity will be directed towards the people who lived then. They will see the seemingly irrational in the past as rational, if explored from the perspective of a different world view. There will be a willingness to explore historical problems and the curiosity to ask valid historical questions. There may be a tendency to view the past as a parallel world which is connected to us by a common humanity; a sense of awe and wonder may be communicated by the pupil. There will be the disposition to look at historical problems from a set of multiple perspectives.

3. **demonstrate historical thinking.** These pupils will be clear abstract thinkers. They will be able to put sources, interpretations and events into a historical context. They will be able to infer and think through historical problems. They will have complex notions of causation. They will be able to make analogies and see anomalies between different historical periods and events. They will make a clear distinction between certainty, probability and possibility. Conclusions will be based on sound reasoning – syllogistic reasoning. They will be able to competently sequence events and classify different historical concepts.

4. **be good language users**. They will posses the language that allows expression of high order thinking. They will possess exploratory language that allows them to express tentative ideas and degrees by which those ideas can be held.

5. **be good reflective learners**. These pupils will reflect upon what it is they have learnt, the process by which they have learnt and where else they can use their learning. There will be, at least tacitly, an understanding that the status of learning is provisional and the process is a dynamic.

This means that we could add to our identification checklist some of these qualities:

- general knowledge about the past

- independent study of the past

- interest and sensitivity to the past

- insight into the past.

Step 3 – General learning qualities

The previous two steps should be within a department's comfort zone. In many senses those stages should allow a department mainly to confirm their instincts about who the able are.

The next two stages are more challenging. They concentrate on more general learning qualities and they allow teachers to begin to view pupils in different ways. As far as qualitative data goes this begins to allow for pupils with potential. These could be pupils who are able and distinctive, but have not demonstrated this in the context of history, or pupils with very large learning abilities that they cannot use at the moment in those classroom settings.

David George, in *The Challenge of the Able Child* (1997), used these criteria to describe the able child. He drew these criteria from the work of Paul Torrance:

- the ability to express emotions easily

- a keen sense of humour

- originality and persistence in problem solving

- curiosity

- high energy levels

- idealism

- artistic interests

- attracted to the unusual, the complex and the mysterious.

How might this manifest itself in the history classroom?

It is the last bullet point which might interest us the most. At its best history is unusual, complex and mysterious. The idea of using introductory stimulus material at the beginning of a lesson, or a good starter activity, is trying to get pupils to look at history in an oblique way. The *Think through history* series produced by

Longman starts each enquiry with a good visual source and an interesting, stimulating and thought-provoking question. For example, in the book *Modern Minds* (Byrom *et al.* 1999), the enquiry on the 'Outbreak of the First World War' starts with the assassination of Archduke Franz Ferdinand and asks the question, 'How did two bullets cause 12 million deaths?' Questions that ask pupils to check their own mini theories and re-evaluate their knowledge can be very powerful.

Sometimes, exploratory and inquiry based work can spin pupils off into different directions than might be expected. This is to be encouraged.

Learning should be fun. The work of Ian Luff is a recent exemplification of this. His work on role-playing, drama and a whole class demonstration show that pupils can be involved, have fun and laugh in a lesson. This builds upon the work of other teacher learners, such as John Nicoll, Chris Jordan and Tim Wood, and David Birt. See Appendix 3.1.

George uses Torrance to develop these characteristics further:

- is full of ideas and sees the relationship between them

- is imaginative and enjoys pretending

- has flexibility of ideas and thoughts

- constructs, builds and then rebuilds

- can cope with several ideas at once

- is always telling others about discoveries or inventions

- likes to do things differently from the norm.

The fourth bullet point might be of particular relevance to us. It is often said that history asks pupils to be critical. It is said that history makes us deconstruct events, sources and interpretations and evaluate them. However, whilst the historian must have a critical eye, the real purpose of history is to reconstruct the past. How often do our pupils have the opportunity to rebuild the past; to take fragmentary pieces of source material and from them produce valid and rational conclusions about the past? We might ask pupils spurious questions about the reliability of a source. We might ask them to deconstruct a source, but can we ask them to reconstruct the past, whilst avoiding the tyranny of 'death by sources A to F'? Consequently we are looking for pupils who have the ability to put things back together, rather than just deconstruct them.

George also suggests negative characteristics:

- stubbornness

- uncooperativeness

- non-participation in certain activities

- low interest in details and indifference to some common conventions and courtesies

- disorganised and sloppy about matters which appear unimportant

- temperamental, demanding and emotional.

These are important to think about. Sometimes we can overcompensate in the gifted and able literature and almost give the impression that every naughty or 'dysfunctional' pupil is secretly able or gifted. This is clearly not the case – however, it is true that these could be used as indicators of underperforming able pupils.

Aspects of creative and productive thinking may be challenging in the classroom. If they are not funnelled in the correct way they may be articulated as a challenge to the teacher, as a challenge to the learning process and as a challenge to the learning product. If the gifted and talented pupils are leaders as well they can act as ringleaders. Taken together with stubbornness, uncooperativeness and a tendency to dismiss aspects of learning in which they are not interested or view as unimportant, then these pupils can be seen as arrogant, annoying and even disruptive.

There is one further challenge for us. Carol Dweck in her book *Self Theories* (1999) argues that a good indicator for future performance is not necessarily a fixed measure at any moment, but the perception the learner has of whether intelligence is fixed or malleable. This is very important for us.

She argues that there are two types of learner. The first kind of learner is performance orientated. Performance orientated learners view intelligence as being fixed. This means that if they perceive their intelligence as being high then they will select those tasks in which they think they will perform well. This is because they see no room for improvement. They view the opportunity of school as not to learn, but to confirm and validate their current position in the class; they wish to maintain their grade average as they do not want to slip.

The other type of learner is the learning orientated learner. This person sees intelligence as being a malleable, changeable quality. They take the view that their performance can be improved over time. They have a tendency to select those tasks that they think will improve their performance and that they will learn the most from. They might make mistakes by which they will learn. Most importantly they see challenge as a prerequisite for successful learning.

It is possible that a good proportion of our able and gifted children might view their intelligence as being fixed. They might be more concerned with performance rather than learning. It is possible that they might value those learning characteristics which have rewarded them in the past. These might include length and depth of work, attention to detail, presentation and neatness of handwriting. It is possible that they might associate successful learning with compliance with what the teacher wants, rather than creativity and high order thinking. It is possible that our gifted and talented learners are not used to challenge. It is possible that they are not used to 'failure'. It is possible that in our teaching and by our interactions we may have to get our gifted and talented pupils to unlearn some learning habits, which so far have been successful for them, so that they may learn new learning habits, which will reward them in the future. This could be emotionally challenging for some.

In concluding this section we may list a further set of characteristics to our checklist:

- skills in group activities

- the ability to express emotions easily

- originality and persistence in problem solving

- curiosity

- attracted to the unusual, the complex and mysterious

and possibly:

- stubbornness

- low interest in details and indifference to some common conventions and courtesies

- disorganised and sloppy about matters which appear unimportant

- temperamental, demanding and emotional

- thought of as 'clever' by their peers

- potentially a leader of their peers.

The checklist can then be constructed along the lines of attributes down the left-hand side and a rating scale along the top ranging from 1 – strong to 5 – weak.

In an ideal world teachers will go through each pupil in each year group individually and rate them against the scale. In the real world there will need to be a sifting process. It is best if staff come to a meeting with a list of 'strong possible' candidates and start from there. Another important point to make is that in the process of constructing such an identification tool in the department it is likely that staff will begin to tentatively identify pupils who are able. Appendix 3.2 provides an exemplar that can be adapted and used by departments.

Step 4 – Widening the scope of what it means to be intelligent and able

We have been examining a model for an able history learner. We have emphasised characteristics which include an expanding knowledge base, divergent and critical thinking, the ability to use language to explain tentative abstract ideas and the capacity to review and reflect. We have begun to place this model in the context of a more general set of characteristics that able pupils have. We shall now examine tools that help us explore intelligence and learning in a broader way. The outcome may be that we find that there are more pupils who could be described as able.

Models of intelligence

Multiple intelligences

Frames of Mind – A Theory of Multiple Intelligences by Howard Gardner is a very well-known and a very powerful book. It was first published in Great Britain in 1983 and gained a widespread currency in educational circles. Its main appeal was that it gave teachers a tool for recognising the achievements and potentials of a wider range of pupils rather than just concentrating on the potentials of a few.

The key idea behind Gardner's work is that intelligence is multi-dimensional. People do not just have one particular type of intelligence; rather they have a **profile of intelligences**. This meant that pupils and teachers no longer had to talk about some pupils being smarter than others or more intelligent than others but instead they could talk about pupils having different intelligence profiles. Our education system has traditionally rewarded pupils who have exhibited strong **linguistic** or **logical–mathematical** intelligences. Notions of being able or weak were dependent on having a particular profile rather than whether there were genuine strengths of intelligence in different areas.

This has meant though that teachers and educationalists have had to revise what it means to be intelligent from a very narrow definition to a far broader one. This means we have to consider how we cater in history for the gifted and talented pupil, who has a very strong spatial intelligence but a weaker linguistic one. It has also given us a far broader tool than we have traditionally used to select the gifted and talented.

We shall now consider Gardner's ideas in more detail. The intelligences can be listed as:

- linguistic intelligence

- musical intelligence

- logical–mathematical intelligence

- spatial intelligence

- bodily–kinaesthetic intelligence

- interpersonal intelligence

- intrapersonal intelligence

- naturalistic intelligence.

What is intriguing is that Gardner introduces each intelligence with a description of somebody who is considered able in that area. However, he does not just simply state what it is they were able to do but conveys a much more empathetic understanding. He at least in part describes what it is like to feel intelligent in that way. The love and aesthetics of number, the intuition that all excellent thinkers feel in their particular area, all these show an excitement in thinking and how the use of a particular intelligence allows high order, nuanced abstract thought.

For example, pupils with a high linguistic intelligence have a love of language and a desire to master it. They tend to give great consideration to the semantics of language. They will use metaphor to explain, understand and analyse the environment around them. They will use language mnemonically and will use language to aid metacognition. They will find it easier to structure and organise their written work. They will find it easier to see the logic and pattern behind written material. To illustrate the world of the linguistic learner Gardner uses the example of the poet. Gardner examines the correspondence between Keith Douglas and T. S. Eliot. In his letters Eliot demonstrates the concern he has for language, choosing the right word to convey his exact meaning. He uses language rhetorically to convince the reader of his meaning and invoke an emotional response. He chooses his metaphors with care. He is able to explain why one word is a better choice than another.

Metacognition

Metacognition is an extremely important aspect of learning. It is more than being aware of what you have learnt, it is also being aware of the processes by which you have learnt. More importantly once those processes are explicit and can be called upon, then we might imagine a child explicitly identifying the thinking 'problem' in front of them and then selecting and blending the most appropriate thinking strategies. On a third level we might expect the pupils to refine those thinking strategies in the light of further reflection and more sophisticated conceptualisation. We would also expect pupils to become increasingly accurate and swift with their thinking. However, for this to work pupils have to be very self-aware.

Gardner advocates that pupils have access to the materials they are studying through a number of entry points as the table below shows:

Multiple intelligences entry points and history examples

Entry point	Historical example
Narrative	The story of the Holocaust
Logical–mathematical	The statistics of the Holocaust
Hands on	Practical presentation using ICT, video etc.
Existential	What does the Holocaust teach us about what it is to be human?
Aesthetic	Poems/art work of the children at Tierzein
Interpersonal/collaborative	Collaborative discussion work on the causes of the Holocaust

The usual outcome of this description of intelligence is to draw up a long list of activities and cross-reference them to the various types of intelligences. This is fine, but it misses a trick I think. The result of this in the classroom is, at best, a variety of activity, but variety for variety's sake. One can see pupils, at the same time, engaged in different activities done at tremendous pace during the lesson, in the hope that at some point they will do something that matches their intelligence. What Gardner actually suggests, and something that most history teachers do, is that they use the entry points when planning the activities in a unit of work.

This is exacerbated if the teacher has done some work on learning styles, particularly if they have read or worked on one to do with sensory disposition such as a **visual**, **auditory** or **kinaesthetic** tool. There almost seems to be an unsaid frustration on the part of the teacher that is analogous with a radio, that they have some learning to transmit and that the pupils are ready to receive but the medium that the teacher ordinarily uses creates interference and that the pupils cannot receive it. If they were to change the medium to synchronise it with how the pupils receive then there would be understanding on both sides.

The result of this would be a more effective transmission model of teaching and learning. It might be more efficient than what was happening before but the net gain is likely to be limited and less than the teacher hoped for. High order thinking and learning may be facilitated by multiple intelligences and learning styles but will not come about from their use in isolation.

Gregorc's analysis

The work of Dr Anthony Gregorc deals with cognitive predilection. He argues that people place themselves on two continuums. One of these is to do with how people perceive information and another on how they order it. Gregorc postulates a continuum moving from **concrete** to **abstract**. Those at the concrete end can only perceive the concrete, the real and what can be physically perceived. Those at the opposite end of the spectrum convert the real into the abstract. They seek mental generalisations from the specific. They find the mental constructions they make to be more real than the physical world around them.

The second continuum refers to how people **order** information. The opposite ends of the spectrum are **sequential** and **random**. Sequential learners have to work in clearly defined structures and systems. These people work in straight lines and in sequence. They cannot parallel think and while they may be precise they are rarely creative. Random thinkers are the opposite. They can make connections between disparate pieces of information. They can run different directions of thinking at the same time. They tend to look for big pictures rather than focused thinking.

Combining the two continuums gives us four types of learner: concrete sequential, concrete random, abstract sequential and abstract random as the diagram shows:

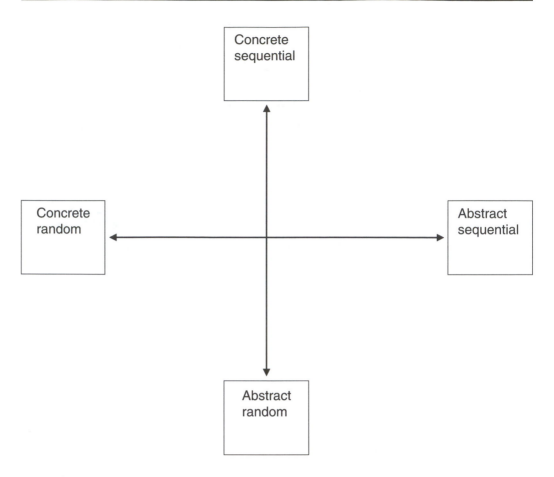

Gregorc's continuums

In *The Teacher's Toolkit* (2002), Paul Ginnis outlines the type of activities and scope for learning that each of the four types of learner enjoy.

These different ways of looking at intelligence and learning styles, Gardner's and Gregorc's, are not exclusive or exhaustive ways of looking at pupils. What they do reinforce is:

- a view that intelligence is not fixed or a single dimension. Therefore any list that is produced of able pupils reflects a particular perception at a fixed point of time. It is not static but dynamic.

- a view that pupil performance can be lifted if there is convergence between the style that the teacher uses to teach and the style the pupil uses to learn. Pupils we might not perceive as able at the moment could be if we varied the learning style in the classroom.

- we should view these learning styles as tools rather than panaceas. They might help promote pupil learning or unlock pupil problems with learning, but they will not automatically do so. They are not a substitute for a good historical enquiry question, or cognitive engagement – the theme of the next chapter.

Abstract Sequential		Concrete Sequential	
Reading	Analysis	Hands on	Maps
Ideas	Evaluation	Concrete examples	Diagrams
Reasoning	Sit down and work	Doing things	Short explanations
Theories	Lectures	Clear-cut objectives	Lists
Debate	Libraries	Structured	Follow rules and conventions
Note taking	Academic work	Step-by-step	Tried and tested methods
Content	Research	Data and figures	Specific answers
Logical	Intellectual	Checklists	Tangible outcomes
Knowledge	Essays	Clear instructions	Methodical
Thinking	Quiet	Attention to detail	Honesty
Individual study	Comprehension	Computers	Field trips
Tests	Philosophy	Charts	Consistency
Structured	Documentation	Outlines	Plans
Mental exercises	Objectivity	Deadlines	
Hypothesising	Comparisons	Manuals	
Vicarious experiences		Real experiences	
Concrete Random		**Abstract Random**	
Problem solving	Creating models	Group work	Intuition
Investigation	Own timetable	Humour	Self-expression
Ingenuity	Up and doing	Games	Own timetable
Finished products	Practical	Movies	Imagination
Choice	Broad guidelines	Non-linear	Peer teaching
Independence	Connected to real world	Relationships	Open-ended tasks
Experiential	Tangible outcomes	Own ideas	Art
Risks	Experiments	Belonging	Discussion
Exploration	Creativity	Music	Drama
Open-ended questions and tasks	Trial and error	Human angle	Media
Big picture, not details	Options	Emotions	Creativity
Curiosity	Challenge	Colour	Fantasy
Originality	Mini-inputs	Spontaneity	Personalised work
Exploration	Games	Flexibility	Poetry
Invention	Flexibility	Stories	Time for reflection
Few restrictions	Lots of resources	Cooperation	Subjectivity
		Visualisation	Movement

Paul Ginnis's description of activities and ways of thinking associated with Gregorc's thinking styles

The model that this chapter has adopted has been to show that:

- high quality learning outcomes need to be planned for. This is not the same as saying that there is a set of Level 5 or 6 activities, but that we should see the attainment target as a set of outcomes that pupils might reach at the end of a journey. Therefore we need to think about what that path might look like for pupils to achieve those outcomes. This also gives us a tool for defining the able – what can they do already?

- their dispositions and attitudes to learning might be a clue to who the able are.

- multiple intelligences, thinking and learning styles may widen the scope and definition of 'able' and may give further clues for identifying the able underachiever.

CHAPTER 4

Classroom provision

- Challenge
- Thinking skills approaches
- Formative assessment strategies

The twenty-first century's visual culture will foster intuitive rather than rational modes of thought, impressions rather than logic, thinking in parallel rather than sequence, pictures rather than paragraphs.

LSRC – as quoted in *Mapping Work on the Future of Teaching and Learning*, Final Report to the General Teaching Council, Peter Rudd, Mark Rickinson, Pauline Benefield (February 2004)

Challenge

Challenge is the key. The largest single benefit for a department focusing on its gifted and talented pupils is that it becomes a way of exploring how to raise the level of cognitive challenge in lessons. Chapter 3 saw how our thinking about who might constitute the able broadens as soon as the tools we use to measure the able broaden from narrow 'cognitive tests'. It broadens even further when we begin to think about those who are **potentially** able.

This chapter mirrors that kind of thinking. It moves from a narrow conception of challenge and instead shows how challenge and thinking can be made more accessible to children. In doing this, lessons become more engaging for a greater number of children with the potential to do well.

We show how one lesson might be transformed and illustrate how, by making changes to the teaching, we can show a qualitative difference to the learning of able pupils. This then leads to sections dealing with more general issues to do with the teaching of the more able. Readers who are familiar with the government's Key Stage 3 National Strategy and articles within the Historical Association's *Teaching History* will recognise many of the points and strategies that will be described in this chapter. This is entirely intentional.

Mr Taylor's lesson

Imagine that you are a head of department or senior manager in a comprehensive school somewhere in England. As part of your duties you monitor the lessons in the history department. Below are the notes of a lesson that you have observed:

The Comprehensive School

Lesson observation – Year 9 class – mixed ability group

Monday 30th January

0900 – (ENTRY) Pupils line up outside the room quietly. They settle down in their places and get out their exercise books and pens.

0907 – (STARTER AND TEACHER EXPOSITION) Mr Taylor starts talking. He has written a key question on the board. It is: 'Why did Germany invade Poland in 1939?' He asks the pupils if they can remember what happened in 1919. He then continues with a narrative account of the inter-war years. His account is punctuated by short questions to the pupils that ask for factual recall. He asks for 'who was', 'when did' type of responses. There are no more than three hands up (all girls) at any one time.

0930 – (DEVELOPMENT) Mr Taylor now has about ten events on the board in the form of a timeline. He has chosen: the Treaty of Versailles, 1919; the Wall Street Crash, 1929; Hitler being made Chancellor of Germany, January 1933; the outbreak of the Spanish Civil War, 1936; the invasion of Abyssinia, 1936; the re-militarisation of the Rhineland, 1936; the invasion of Czechoslovakia and the Munich Crisis, 1938; the German–Soviet Non-Aggression Pact, 1939; and the Anglo-French Guarantee of Polish borders, 1939. He asks the pupils to copy the timeline into their books.

0935 – (EXTENSION) Mr Taylor asks the pupils to stop. Some have not yet finished. He asks them to use their textbooks to write a short paragraph about each of the events on the timeline.

The pupils begin this task. You move around the class. The pupils engage with the task to begin with, but after about five minutes some of the pupils are distracted. You take this opportunity to look at the exercise books. The books are marked every two weeks, in line with departmental and school policy. He has given the pieces of work a mark out of ten and a comment. The most typical types of comment ask pupils to add more detail, to complete work or there is a remark about presentation.

0950 – (PLENARY) Mr Taylor calls the class together and he asks them why they think that Germany invaded Poland in 1939. Which of the events on the board was the most important in determining why war broke out? A few pupils respond. They mainly say that the war broke out because Hitler came to power in 1933, or because the Treaty of Versailles was bad. Mr Taylor mutters something about Hitler's actions being consistent with traditional German foreign policy and then asks the pupils to pack their books away.

You look at the notes with dismay. This is certainly not a good lesson. Three years ago it might have been placed by Ofsted in a satisfactory category; now it would be definitely struggling. This is a lesson where the practitioner has not engaged with the articles and ideas contained in the Historical Association's *Teaching History* or the Key Stage 3 National Strategy.

In some ways this might be seen as a positive lesson:

- The pupils were behaving in an orderly fashion.

- There was a lot of detail covered in the lesson.

- There was a key historical question which focused on causation.

However, there are a number of concerns that are making this lesson weaker:

- The beginning of the lesson is focusing on management and recall of information rather than 'big picture' learning, or presenting learning as a problem or puzzle to be solved and engage pupils with.

- There is a lot of historical content that is being treated as information. Pupils need to know their history, but knowing involves more than simply reciting isolated facts. **At the very least** it involves knowing the significance of a piece of information and where it fits into a broader analysis or narrative.

- The task that the pupils are involved in is very low level. A copying task does not promote learning. At best it could be said that the teacher is providing pupils with a record to revise from. One suspects that such an activity is also provided because of misconceptions of classroom management.

- Assessment may be complying with school policy but is having little impact on pupil learning.

- Few pupils could offer reasons for the outbreak of war in 1939, yet this was the objective of the lesson.

The key to this is to understand that in this lesson it is the teacher who has done the thinking not the pupils. In this lesson the teacher has:

- thought through the context of the lesson

- determined the significance of the individual events

- selected the events that he wants the pupils to recall

- thought that pupils need to know the facts before they can analyse them

- equated depth of coverage with depth of learning.

By doing this the teacher is operating in a transmission mode. He considers that he has the knowledge and all he has to do is tell the pupils what it is that he knows.

Constructing knowledge or disseminating it?

Alternatively a teacher who is working to *constructivist* principles recognises:

- There is a dialogue between what the pupil already knows and new learning. Therefore the starting point for the teacher needs to be the understanding and knowledge that the pupils already have.

- That pupils have to internalise new information – in other words they have to organise it as well as process it.

- That organisation is not done in isolation. New information has to be integrated with existing knowledge structures – this means that pupils have to revise what they knew already in the light of what they have learnt as well as determine the significance of what they have just learnt by comparing it to what they knew already. Learning discrete pieces of information (facts) might help pupils pass a particular test, but for deeper learning this information has to be accommodated into existing structures.

- Cognitive conflict – tension in their learning. Pupils learn best where there is cognitive dissonance. This means that pupils are presented with information that they have to reconcile. It makes them suffer 'mental anguish'. It will require mental effort to think their way through the material.

- The teacher will be planning for pupil misconceptions. In lessons these misconceptions will be made explicit and worked through by the pupils.

- Metacognition – pupils actually reflecting upon the process of their thinking becomes crucial. It will enable pupils to be better learners and more self-aware learners as they proceed. They will become more aware of what it means to study history and to think historically.

Change the lesson to change the learning

This next section will analyse parts of the lesson and show how individual sections of it could be changed to make the lesson more cognitively engaging.

Purposeful beginnings: from managing the pupils to priming the learning

The beginnings of lessons are prime time for learning and all too often this is a time that can be dominated by lesson administration. Pupils, and **especially the more able**, need to be engaged with their learning, to be puzzled, intrigued by the problem set before them and to relate this to their wider learning. This will help pupils to think through the material, create tension in their learning and begin to look at the material critically.

Initial stimulus material and starter activities provide two tools that the history teacher can use to make their lessons more challenging.

In his book *Reflective Teaching of History, 11–18* (2002), Robert Phillips discusses the notion of using initial stimulus material in history lessons. He argues there are three broad purposes to using initial stimulus material:

- the ways in which historical material can be organised to stimulate interest and curiosity

- the establishment of a line of enquiry of posing a hypothesis about a historical issue by the key question or a series of questions

- the means by which we can outline aims and objectives in a clever, meaningful way.

He discusses the use of the famous Dutch print of the execution of Charles I in introducing the English Civil War. Even though he wanted pupils to think about causation (that is, why did war break out in 1642?) his starting point was to look at the execution in 1649. By showing the print and by getting the pupils to analyse it to think about what might be going on, to identify its key parts, to think about its significance, he was activating pupils' curiosity. He was getting them to think about the significance of what it was that they would be investigating. An important aspect of this was that the pupils had no prior knowledge of the English Civil War. Therefore, the pupils were **speculating** and **hypothesising** what the

The execution of Charles I

significance of the painting might be, rather than recalling the actual. This meant that pupils were thinking, and trying to work things out.

It is important at this juncture to emphasise two points:

1. It is not necessary to produce a correct answer at this stage. It will be more fruitful to allow several working hypotheses or possibilities. The teacher should not close down thinking or discard 'incorrect' suggestions.

2. These initial ideas must not be left in 'limbo' during the remainder of the lesson. If this were to happen then the pupils have simply engaged in idle speculation of an unhistorical nature. The teacher could refer to pupils' initial ideas as the lesson progressed and ask them to reflect on their initial thoughts and which they now consider to be the most likely and why.

This is a higher level of cognitive challenge than simply recalling events. An interesting possibility of using Introductory Stimulus Material (ISM) is that it can be used to make the objectives, which are set in the lesson, more real. It can give a sense of exploration to the lesson. It might mean that the ISM is revisited, reviewed and reflected upon at the end of the lesson. Pupils might decide which lines of enquiry now seem to be more promising and which ideas seem to be more powerful. This gives a nice circular structure to the lesson.

Creating challenge with initial stimulus materials

Puzzles can be created and work best when pupils:

- are asked to look at material from an oblique perspective

- find that their assumptions about the past are challenged

- look at the unusual

- are asked to speculate and predict

- discover that conflict is created between what they might have expected to have happened with what actually happened.

Consider, for example, what the impact on pupil learning might have been if Mr Taylor had shown his pupils the famous cartoon: 'Peace and Future Cannon Fodder'.

Once this cartoon has been analysed by pupils in groups with prompts, or as a 'layers of inference diagram' as to who the main figures were and the significance of the weeping boy, they can then begin to use it as stimulus to consider the following questions:

- Why do you think some people were saying in 1919 that war might break out twenty years later?

'Peace and Future Cannon Fodder'

● Do you think that because some people were saying in 1919 that war might happen later that the Treaty of Versailles caused Hitler to invade Poland in 1939?

● Do you think that the cartoon means that the outbreak of war in 1939 was inevitable?

These are three tricky questions! Yet given enough thinking time, perhaps considering their answers in groups and being encouraged by the use of tentative language, most classes could begin to speculate on those questions. To answer those questions pupils will:

● be drawing on their prior knowledge of the period. What do they know about the Treaty of Versailles, what else have they learnt, either formally in lessons or informally via the media? Will they mention Hitler; will some have heard of appeasement?

● begin to identify possible reasons. The questions that are being asked are to do with causation. This means that pupils are already beginning to draw upon notions of causation that they have developed from other lessons. This is reinforced by the use of a key question approach.

● have to think about possible relationships between possible causes. Is there inevitability; have we started to make distinctions between long term and short term causes; will they begin to express tentative ideas, not expressed in adult language, about **direct** and **indirect** causes or their **necessity** or **sufficiency**?

It is important to emphasise that pupils are not giving definite answers – they are speculating. They are beginning to think their way through the issues that are going to be tackled in the main part of the lesson. This means that the teacher does not have to spend a long time in teasing out 'right' answers from pupils but spends the time generating a set of possible or plausible responses from them.

This strikes a resonance with the Key Stage 3 National Strategy's notion of starter activities. In this module teachers are asked to explore the idea of having an activity at the start of the lesson to engage pupils and prepare them for the main part of the lesson. It argues that the key characteristics of a starter activity are:

- essentially active in nature – getting the lesson off to a flying start

- a focus on an appropriately demanding pace in thinking and learning rather than the business of activity

- providing thought-provoking and engaging beginnings to lessons

- not 'compulsory' but can add greatly to a lesson's effectiveness

- a tool to create lively introductions – the first stage in meeting the key lesson objectives

- a tool for 'little and often' teaching of knowledge and skills

- a way of planning a sequence of discrete units to build knowledge, understanding and motivation over a series of lessons

- a way of exploiting prime learning time – pupils are often at their most receptive at the beginning of lessons and concentration levels are high, yet this time is often devoted to administrative and organisational tasks.

In this sense initial stimulus material can be seen as a subset of a wider notion of starter activities. In the foundation subjects 'starters' module, participants are asked to perform a starter activity themselves by placing a number of starter activities on a continuum. The perceived level of challenge determined their place on the continuum. Taking some of the appropriate activities we can make further suggestions for Mr Taylor's starter:

1. Pupils are placed in groups and given five pieces of information on cards – a picture of Hitler at a rally, a picture of a Panzer II tank, a picture of Chamberlain waving a piece of paper on his return from Munich, the 'Peace and Future Cannon Fodder' cartoon and a written description of the destruction of Guernica. They have to come up with possible ways of saying what these pieces of information have in common. They then have to select two pieces of information and explore possible links between them before repeating the process with three pieces of information.

2. Pupils are placed in groups and are given a large sheet of sugar paper, in the centre of which are written the words 'Outbreak of World War 2 – September 3rd 1939'. Pupils then have a set time limit in which to brainstorm prior knowledge and ideas that they associate with this event. After a set period of time they could look at other groups' work. They could walk around with a set of Post-it notes and annotate the work of others – what they agree with, what they didn't know and what they would like the other group to check or think about.

3. Pupils are placed in groups. They are given two sets of colour-coded cards. One set specifies the events (without dates). The second provides descriptions of the events. Pupils are asked first to match what they consider to be the correct events with the definitions, then to consider what the correct sequence of events might be. This could be a particularly cunning starter. The key to making this work is to plan the phrasing of the description of the events very carefully. From this pupils should not just be able to associate event and description but give hints as to its relationship with other events and its significance. This will allow the pupils to sequence these events effectively. The second way to use this starter effectively when taking feedback from the pupils is **not to generate the right answer**. This defeats the entire purpose of doing this as a starter activity. Instead the teacher should generate a tentative answer, which will be incorrect in places – in fact it is better if it is incorrect in places. This means that as the story unfolds between 1919 and 1939, pupils can be asked to correct their answers and reflect upon the differences between what happened and what they thought happened and explore the difference in reasoning between the two. This could be done as a continuous process or as part of a plenary at the end.

4. Pupils are asked to compare and contrast two short quotes on the causes of the Second World War – one written by A. J. P. Taylor and the other by R. J. Overy. How do these two short statements compare with each other – how are they similar and how are they different? Can they use this to then generate three to five questions that would help them understand the causes of the Second World War better?

If Mr Taylor had a lesson that focused upon interpretations, could he have shown a short video clip and asked pupils to comment upon how an event has been interpreted?
   Examples could include:

-   *Oliver* for conditions in workhouses and Victorian England

-   *Saving Private Ryan* and *The Longest Day* – how do they differ in their interpretation of the D-Day landings?

-   *The Battle of Britain* – a good film to use when exploring notions of the Blitz Spirit and Britain's wartime role.

Managing starter activities

When using a **starter** activity or using **initial stimulus material** the following should be borne in mind:

- Establish routines and expectations that the starter is an activity, which can be done with minimal teacher input. Can you tell the pupils that there is a starter waiting for them whilst they are outside the classroom waiting to come in? Can you make the convention explicit that the starter is waiting for them and they begin it whilst you are calling the register? Can you have the explicit convention that stragglers and latecomers come in and join a group?

- Remember that with a starter, main part of the lesson and plenary, these are not discrete activities that each have a specific beginning, middle and end, but three overlapping, interconnecting lesson episodes that are distinguished by getting the pupils to think in different ways: **starter and speculation of learning**; **main part and assimilation of learning**; **plenary and reflection of learning**. This means that with the starter activity you do not have to correct every misconception or every point that the pupils get wrong. Instead later on in the lesson you might want to refer back to what pupils thought in the starter activity and ask them to make their own corrections or ask them how their thinking has changed and why.

- Deal promptly with feedback from pupils and keep promptly to timings.

- Plan explicitly the questions you wish to ask the pupils in the class. Normally about three is just right. Plan so that the questions stimulate the kind of thinking that you want from pupils.

Why do this?

It is important to do this:

- to engage the pupils with purposeful historical activity at the beginning of the lesson

- to inject a sense of high expectation and challenge at the beginning of a lesson sequence

- to facilitate the construction of knowledge, understanding and meaning in a lesson by demanding that pupils construct a working hypothesis or speculate to generate a set of ideas that can be reviewed and refined as the lesson progresses.

Lesson starters and the able child

An argument has been put forward for the potential use of starter activities in lessons. However, the examples that have been used have been what might loosely be termed high challenge starters. In the identification chapter it was argued that gifted and talented pupils needed increased levels of challenge and that they should be introduced to and helped to develop higher levels of thinking. The starter can be one tool to do this. It can introduce early levels of challenge. It can encourage our able and talented children to speculate and predict early in a lesson. It can allow pupils to be creative.

Where to get lesson starter materials from

As can be appreciated these lesson starter materials could take a lot of preparation. One could imagine classes consuming quantities of information and resources. Where can we get further help from?

- It is far better to plan collaboratively within the department and to pass resources and ideas on. This is the only sustainable way of doing this. Individual teachers will very quickly get swamped.

- Audit the textbooks that you have already. Are there juicy, intriguing and mysterious sources that can be used as stimulus material?

- Within your video resources do you have small sections of documentary or movie footage that could be used?

- Use written fiction material. Dickens gives a colourful account of Victorian England, for example. Stories about Robin Hood can be equally useful, etc.

- The internet, as ever, contains a wealth of useful material.

- Can you build up a repertoire of activities? Badger Publishing, for example, have produced a booklet of starter activities that have matched activities to lessons in the QCA schemes of work. This may be a useful starting point.

- Through departmental meetings could you produce your own booklet of useful strategies that work with your children – can these be shared and swapped with other departments in the school?

- Can you work with your LA's Secondary Strategy Consultant to develop a repertoire of starter activities?

What do you think the impact on pupil learning might have been for the entire class, and specifically the able child within the class, if your observation notes on Mr Taylor's lesson had read:

0900 (ENTRY) – Pupils enter the room. They settle down in their places and get out their exercise books and pens.

(STARTER) On the whiteboard is written the key question: 'Why did Germany invade Poland in 1939?' Projected onto it is the 'Peace and Future Cannon Fodder' cartoon. Pupils are asked to identify the people they can see in the picture, identify where the cartoon is set and asked to speculate why the boy is crying. As they are discussing this in pairs, Mr Taylor calls the register. After five minutes he asks pupils to think about these three questions: Why do you think some people were saying in 1919 that war might break out twenty years later? Do you think that because some people were saying in 1919 that war might happen later that the Treaty of Versailles caused Hitler to invade Poland in 1939? Do you think that the cartoon means that the outbreak of war in 1939 was inevitable? Some pupils struggled with the questions. Some gave some tentative answers. Most pupils really began to make the links between the Treaty of Versailles and what happened later. A few pupils were able to challenge this. They wondered whether a link could last that long. Would it be as important as something that happened later? They urged caution to their peers saying that they needed to find out more before they could start giving individual causes weight.

Sharing learning intentions (objectives)

We share learning intentions with pupils for the following reasons:

- to make it explicit to pupils what it is they are learning

- to help pupils distinguish what they are learning from what they are doing

- to provide a starting point for pupil reflection of progress in a lesson

- to provide a focus for both teacher and pupil during the lesson so that dialogue between teacher, pupil and their learning can be created

- to provide a starting point for pupils to construct their own learning.

Learning intentions are not:

- a list of activities

- a list of accomplishments that pupils will **produce**

- the answers

- a meaningless list of aspirations

- referred to only once during a lesson

- inert

- a tick list

- a restrictive list of the only things that will be learnt in a lesson

- a tool for judging teachers – teachers and pupils will not have 'failed' if the objectives have not been reached.

What does this mean?

Sharing learning objectives provides an explicit way of communicating to pupils what it is they are learning so that they can distinguish between the busyness of activity and the learning that is taking place. If we want pupils to reflect and evaluate the extent of their learning and the processes they used then they need to know what it is they are supposed to be learning. It is that simple and everything else is just the means by which that happens. It also gives us a useful rule of thumb – if the learning intention you are communicating to the pupils will not help them focus on what it is you want them to learn, then don't do it.

The difference between learning intentions and learning outcomes

A **learning intention** is what it is you want the pupils to learn.
A **learning outcome** is what pupils will demonstrate to show what it is they have learnt.

All pupils should have the same learning intention. You would expect all pupils in a class to be learning the same thing. However, we know that pupils will differ in their achievements. Therefore, the intention in the class will not differ, but the outcomes will. QCA schemes of work use the model of all pupils will, most pupils should, some pupils could for their outcomes. This seems to me to be an entirely appropriate model to use.

Framing objectives for history lessons

The Key Stage 3 National Strategy Foundation Subjects Unit 3 provides us with a set of writing stems to use when framing objectives.

By the end of this lesson pupils will:

- **Know that** . . . (knowledge: factual information, for example names, places, symbols, formulae, events.)

- **Develop/be able to** . . . (skills: using knowledge, applying techniques, analysing information etc.)

- **Understand how/why** . . . (understanding: concepts, reasons, effects, principles, processes, etc.)

- **Develop/be aware of** . . . (attitudes and values: empathy, caring sensitivity towards social issues, feelings, moral issues, etc.)

Objectives may also focus on how pupils learn.

This provides us with a starting point. There is a clear distinction between the different areas of learning. There is no need to write an objective for every stem for every lesson. There is no need to write an objective for everything that the pupils could possibly learn. **You are identifying the focus of the learning of the lesson to aid reflection later.** Golden rules for writing and using lesson objectives include:

- Write them in pupil-friendly language.

- Shirley Clarke (2005) argues that learning intentions should be content free. Therefore 'identify the causes of the Second World War' should, as a learning intention, read 'identify causes' and the Second World War is simply the context for a wider, more general set of historical thinking – that of being able to identify a cause.

- Go through them with the pupils in the lesson and check for understanding.

- Make them as precise as possible. Simply writing the word 'interpretations' on the board as an objective is not very useful.

- Make the objectives manageable. Writing 'revise the Norman Conquest', or 'know the names of all the Kings in the Stuart dynasty' does not really help anyone.

- Give due consideration to writing objectives about how pupils learn.

The problem with 'understanding'

Experience tells us that teachers are generally good at generating objectives based around knowledge. However, it is harder to write objectives based around understanding. At this point they tend to become too general and unhelpful to pupils. The stem 'understand', by itself, does not generate objectives which unpack the kind of thinking which pupils are required to make to help them understand. However, help is at hand. Unit 3 of the whole school materials – Assessment for Learning – contains a useful grid of words, which describe pupil thinking in ascending levels of difficulty. These help unpack understanding with more precision. See Appendix 4.1 'Vocabulary for framing learning objectives and expected learning outcomes'. This document gives a useful framework for developing progressively more challenging lesson objectives.

Secondly it could be argued that the learning focus for a lesson should be based around one of the key elements of the National Curriculum:

- key features of the past

- making connections between periods and in between periods

- historical significance

- historical interpretations

- historical enquiry

- historical trends.

We would encourage teachers to use the grid as a starting point and think about the precise requirements of the key elements and see if the grid can help them chart progression of learning.

A key question approach

The most recent advocates of the key question approach are Christine Counsell and Michael Riley. There are similarities with the use of learning intentions. They agree:

- that pupils should be told the learning intention for the lesson

- that pupils should be encouraged to reflect upon their responses to the learning intention

- that learning intentions can be used to plan for, or create a pathway of progression, through a unit of work, school year or key stage.

However, they would argue that the use of key questions as a way of sharing learning intentions has a number of advantages.

Key questions can be used to engage pupils and make them think in ways that objectives cannot. This is heavily dependent upon how the questions are phrased. 'Why did people become Protestants?' is a question that will elicit predictable answers. However the question 'Why didn't everybody become Protestants?' is a question which will take pupil learning in unpredictable directions and cause cognitive conflict so that pupils simply think a lot harder. Devising these questions requires a good deal of struggle as Jamie Byrom and Michael Riley showed in their article 'Professional wrestling in the history department: a case study in planning the teaching of the British Empire at Key Stage 3', which appeared in the *Empire* edition of *Teaching History* (Issue 112, September 2003).

A good history department will consider some or all the following questions when devising a unit or scheme of work.

- Why are we asking them to study this?
- What do we really want the pupils to get better at here?
- How on earth do we decide what to leave out?
- Yes, but can we really leave that bit out?
- This is difficult, but important – how do we make it accessible?
- This is important but boring – how can we make it more enjoyable?
- How does this work build on earlier work?
- How does this work prepare for later work?
- Are we asking enough of them?
- Are we asking too much of them?
- We know exactly what they will get wrong here – but what can we do about it?
- How can we add variety to help different types of learner?
- How can we stop all this getting fragmented?
- What can we get them to do to show their progress?
- How can we help them to know how they are getting better?
- How do we make it to the end of term?

Key questions can be used to create pathways for progression through material. They can also be used as a way to create understanding through historical content, as pupils are made explicitly aware of the themes they have already examined. This knowledge can be used to assimilate new content, it can help pupils generate their own questions and help pupils detect anomaly and analogy. In other words by using key questions to actively think their way through the material and to create a dialogue with it, pupils understand it better.

Implications for gifted and talented pupils

Able pupils benefit, like all other pupils, by having the learning intentions of the lessons shared with them. Both the use of lesson objectives and key questions are useful ways of doing this. Variety is the key.

Do use key questions if:

- You intend to have a genuine exploratory/investigative lesson. There is nothing worse than a teacher posing a question and then answering it.

- You intend to use questions which are genuinely thought-provoking.

- You intend to allow time in the lesson for pupils to answer the question – however tentative that answer might be.

- You intend pupils to draw analogies and detect anomalies with previous content.

- You intend to use content as a stimulus and a way of engaging the pupils.

- You structure your Key Stage 3/4 course around more progressively challenging historical questions that require pupils to make explicit comparisons between those questions. Ideally they should be able to recognise that different questions require different historical thinking. In other words they should be able to determine which questions require them to think about causation etc.

Do use lesson objectives if:

- You want to emphasise the process of **how** pupils learn as well as **what** they learn.

- You want to emphasise other aspects of learning which are not necessarily exemplified by content.

- The lesson does not lend itself to an exploratory mode.

What do you think the impact on pupil learning might have been now for the entire class, and specifically the able child within the class, if your observation notes on Mr Taylor's lesson had read:

> 0910 (Beginning of teacher exposition) – Mr Taylor introduces the pupils to the learning objectives for the lesson. He tells the pupils that:
> 'We are learning to:
>
> - describe the key events between 1919 and 1939
>
> - identify the causes of World War Two

- understand how the causes interact and relate with each other.'

Mr Taylor then asks the children what they think they might have to do in the lesson to achieve those objectives. He checks that they understand, or at the very least think about, the cognitive stems of describe and identify and possible ways of interaction. Having established the learning objectives he proceeds to an explanation of the content and task:

- explore how we can determine the significance of the different causes.

Question and intervention

Questioning is probably one of the most important teaching skills there are. It is the way that we interact with pupils and it governs the dialogue and discourse within the classroom. It is the easiest way to create challenge in the classroom. It is also the easiest way to depress it.

Teachers also instinctively know that this is an area of pedagogy that could do with sharpening. There has been a good deal of research that has got into the public domain that shows:

- Teachers ask too many questions.

- Teachers ask too many of the wrong questions. If we were to classify the questions asked of pupils by their teachers into the following groups: managerial; knowledge recall; cognitive/thinking questions then the proportion of the types of questions that teachers would ask would be 54%, 42% and 4% respectively.

- Teachers do not give pupils enough time to think before they expect an answer.

- Teachers do not give enough time for pupils to speak.

- Teachers do not always structure the questions they are asking.

- Pupils are not always allowed to ask questions.

- Sometimes questions are asked, when an alternative form of interaction will be more appropriate.

There are a number of good classroom conventions that can be used to help combat this problem:

- A no-hands rule. We know that sometimes in the classroom, it is only a few pupils who volunteer to answer questions. Sometimes it can appear that a conversation is taking place between the teacher and only one or two other pupils. Instead the teacher should direct questioning, around the class. This has the advantage of concentrating the minds of the pupils. It establishes the expectation that all should be able to offer an answer. It also might mean that the teacher can make sure that all pupils have the opportunity to answer questions.

- The use of tentative language. Sometimes the questions we ask depress pupil responses. Consider the following. A teacher asks his Year 7 history class: 'Who was crowned king on Christmas Day in 1066?' At first glance, this question may seem a very easy question to answer. However, it is quite a risky situation for the pupils. Their answers will simply be right or wrong. If they are unsure of the answer, they know they have a 50% chance of being wrong. There is little opportunity to reason the answer, and a guess may make them seem foolish. If on the other hand, they know that the answer is William the Conqueror then it may seem a trivial question to answer. They know the answer, they know the teacher knows the answer, therefore what is the virtue in answering the question? It is not simply this particular example which works in this particular way. Consider the following questions: between what years did King Stephen reign; who was the German chancellor after Bethmann-Hollweg; where did Hernan Cortes land in Mexico? All these questions are more difficult. But the pupil response is to work in the same way. These questions are ridiculously easy if you know the answer and difficult if you do not. A way to work around this is to ask questions which involve the use of tentative language. Specifically, if you use the words may, might, think when questions are phrased then pupils seem to consider these as giving them permission to guess.

- Snowballing. Sometimes the questions we ask pupils might be speculative or generative in nature. In this instance we might want pupils to come up with as many ideas they can. But this may be beyond them acting as a single person. Snowballing is a way of generating ideas. After the question has been asked pupils are required to note down one or two possible answers. They then show their ideas to the person sitting next to them. They copy each other's ideas and add one or two extra ideas between them. Next each pair shows their ideas to another pair. Each pair records any ideas that they have not generated so far and generates a few further responses as a group. Each pupil will now have a range of possible responses in front of them, so now the teacher can ask their questions using a no hands rule.

- Using the convention of think time. Wragg and Brown (2001) record that the average time from a teacher asking a question to either receiving an answer or asking the question again is less than one second. If we have defined pace in such a way then it is unlikely that we will be able to ask questions which require more than one word answers. If we are planning on asking questions which require pupils to think harder, then they need the time to think. We should say to pupils that they have one or two seconds to think of an answer before the teacher will take responses.

- Allow pupils to ask their own questions. In groups provide them with a set of information and ask them what kinds of questions this information might generate.

- Ask fewer, planned, increasingly more challenging questions. Having three key questions in mind to ask pupils at the beginning of a lesson is about right.

Asking good historical questions

Tim Lomas wrote an excellent pamphlet called *Teaching and Assessing Historical Understanding* for the Historical Association in 1990. The focus of the pamphlet was generating questions for assessment purposes. A real advantage of the pamphlet was that it began to associate questions with different cognitive domains within history. Therefore, there are questions for dealing with causation, significance, continuity and change, key features of the past, etc. We can develop this to focus on the National Curriculum attainment targets and how they might work in the classroom. We ought to consider the questions below as main planning questions. In actual classrooms we may adapt them, simplify them and break them down as appropriate. Lack of space precludes examining every area, but as an example here are some questions which may be useful when we examine causation.

Good questions regarding causation

What we want children to do is to identify causes, categorise them by their function, explore the relationships between them and determine the importance of their impact. Questions that help pupils do this include:

Offering and categorising reasons:

Why do you think Germany invaded Poland in September 1939?

Which of the following do you think are reasons for Germany invading Poland in 1939?

Which of the following do you think are not reasons for Germany invading Poland in 1939?

What do you think were the long term/short term/direct/indirect causes of the Second World War?

What makes you think that these causes are long term/short term/direct/indirect **rather than** long term/short term/direct/indirect causes?

Why do you think other people might put these causes into different categories?

Exploring relationships between causes:

How might the Treaty of Versailles **and the rise of Hitler relate with each other?**

How do you think the Treaty of Versailles **allowed the other causes to develop?**

If the Treaty of Versailles **happened** twenty years **previously then why do you think it is a cause of** the Second World War?

If the Treaty of Versailles **had not occurred then would** the Second World War **have happened anyway?**

Thinking about importance:

Why might the Treaty of Versailles **be an important cause?**

> **Do you think** the Treaty of Versailles **was a more important cause** than appeasement in causing the Second World War?
>
> **If** Chamberlain had not appeased Hitler in 1938 then **do you think** the Second World War **would still have occurred**?
>
> **Why might** appeasement **be a more important cause than** the Treaty of Versailles?
>
> **If** the Treaty of Versailles **was more important than** appeasement does **this mean it was more important than** the Anschluss?
>
> **Do you think that it is more important to consider** how the economy affected people **rather than** events happening between countries?
>
> **Why do you think other people have a different opinion to you?**

Good questions are thought-provoking. It is hard to pin down why a particular question is more thought-provoking than another but here are some general principles:

1. Pupils are asked questions from different perspectives than they are used to.

2. The teacher uses language that the pupils need to unpack – i.e. inevitable, must, it would have wouldn't it.

3. Questions where pupils are asked to weigh up possibilities and asked to distinguish between probable and possible.

4. Questions which cause cognitive dissonance.

5. Questions which elicit exceptions and their significance.

What do you think the impact on pupil learning might have been now for the entire class, and specifically the able child within the class, if your observation notes on Mr Taylor's lesson had read:

> 0915 – Instead of launching into a discrete question and answer episode Mr Taylor gave an explanation of the events and then a set of instructions regarding the task. In other words instead of having a question and answer episode at the beginning of a lesson – which is normally a warm-up or recall of events – the kind of cognitive questioning we have been talking about tends to happen more at the end of the lesson.

Beating 'neat nonsense' – constructing the learning in the main part of the lesson

In Mr Taylor's lesson the pupils are doing work which at best might be described as a comprehension exercise. There is an initial sequencing activity and then pupils are asked to make summaries and notes. There is nothing inherently wrong with this approach. These activities can be used as a vehicle for pupil thinking and the aggregation of knowledge can aid progression. However, in this instance it seems that Mr Taylor is not supporting pupil learning in that way.

Instead pupils seem to be doing work which is essentially recording information. Pupils are not critically engaged with it and there does seem to be a feeling that pupils are not cognitively engaged with the materials. In this next section we shall see how teachers can increase the levels of challenge in a lesson and support pupil learning.

Pupil learning: more challenging or more difficult?

Here is a short list of some of the things that history teachers can do to make work more appropriate for gifted and talented pupils:

1. Give able pupils a wider range of sources to work with.

2. Ask able pupils questions with higher demands of thinking.

3. Ask able pupils questions which encourage them to predict, speculate and hypothesise.

4. Give able pupils the same number of sources as everybody else but make theirs longer.

5. Give able pupils a tighter time limit.

6. Give able pupils less of a literacy scaffold.

7. Insist on greater precision from able pupils.

8. Insist on neater work from able pupils.

9. Demand able pupils problem-solve and reach their own conclusions.

10. Ask able pupils to identify patterns in historical data.

11. Ask able pupils to reach a substantiated judgement based on a number of conflicting sources.

12. Ask able pupils to reflect on and regulate their own thinking.

If you had to classify those statements into two groups, group one with the heading of increasing pupil challenge, and group two with the heading of making things more difficult for pupils, how would you separate the statements? What criteria would you use for challenge and which for difficulty? Do you think we, as history teachers, confuse the two meanings?

Points 1, 4, 5, 6, 7 and 8 are activities, which might make things more difficult for pupils.

Points 1 and 4 equate the idea that giving pupils more of the same means that they will be working better. It implies able pupils will be producing longer answers than the others. This is obviously not the case. If the pupils are being asked some comprehension questions in the guise of history then that is what they are being asked to do regardless of how many sources they have been given or the complexity of these. This is not the same as providing pupils with enough information to complete a complex task. This is not the same as providing pupils with longer sources so that they can 'connect' with the past as Christine Counsell wonderfully illustrates in her book, *History and Literacy in Year 7* (2004).

The multi-dimensional nature of challenge

We might, if we were visual learners, imagine challenge as being a four-dimensional graph. On one dimension might be the axis labelled pupil thinking, the next axis might be labelled the literacy demand of the task, the next axis might be labelled knowledge and the fourth axis might be labelled support.

What has been argued is that able and gifted pupils in history need to think harder. They need to move away from description to explanation and further still into analytical work. Hence, what will be of the greatest use to the pupils are tasks that get them to think harder. If they are exposed simply to tasks which require them to read more, record more, do it more accurately and spell it properly they will not achieve higher levels in the National Curriculum, GCSE or indeed enjoy the subject. Hence this thinking axis is the most critical. However, it needs qualification. All the axes are interlinked. We have all seen, or perhaps used, activities which superficially require pupils to think harder but

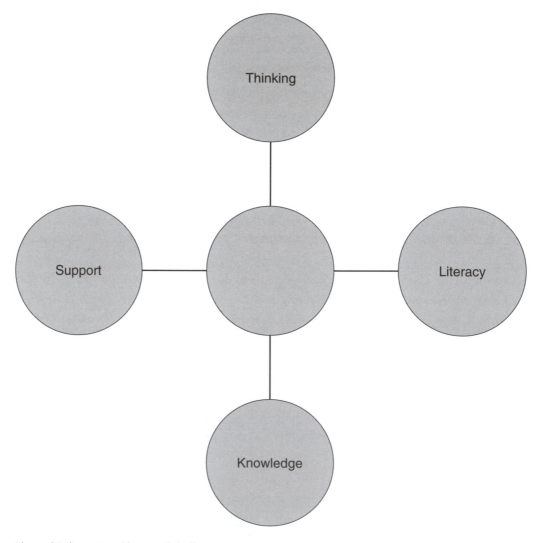

The multi-dimensional layers of challenge

do not give them enough contextual information to work with. This then involves the pupils in guessing. There needs to be appropriate amounts of knowledge for the pupils so that they can analyse. However, simply giving pupils lots of information will not automatically lead pupils to higher understanding and more sophisticated thinking. In this sense it can be said that providing able pupils with extra or increasingly difficult information can be a necessary requirement to help them think at appropriate levels, but by itself it will not be sufficient to ensure it.

Richard Harris has written an extremely useful article on challenge and how to make it accessible to pupils – 'Does differentiation have to mean different?' (*Teaching History* 118, March 2005). In this article he explores how challenge and thinking can be made accessible to pupils so that more can achieve than would otherwise be the case. It really is an important read.

Tools for helping us think about challenge

Bloom's taxonomy

Benjamin Bloom and his associates, writing in the 1950s, examined a great many questions and activities that teachers were using in the United States. They then categorised them and arranged them in order of increasing challenge. This ranking, or topography, became known commonly as Bloom's taxonomy. It is a handy tool that we can use because it is simple and can give an **indication** of the level of challenge that is present.

Bloom's taxonomy reads as:

- **Knowledge** – We might think of this as being common to description and identification. It is asking pupils to recall a discrete fact, identify a concept, or describe an object without giving any indication that they understand, or comprehend, the answer. *For example: who became king on Christmas Day in 1066; between what years did King Stephen reign; what name did the Sioux Indians give to the buffalo?* These questions are precise, quick to ask and answer and useful for checking pupils' recall of information.

- **Comprehension** – Pupils demonstrate passive understanding. They are required to extract information, show simple understanding of definitions and give simple reasons. *For example: why did the Normans invade England; what do we mean by feudalism; how does this source tell us that the Sioux were able to survive the winter?*

- **Application** – This requires pupils to predict, speculate, compare similarities and differences and take their learning from one context to another. It is characterised by 'if . . . then' or 'should . . . could' types of questions. *For example: if William had invaded England earlier in the year do you think that he would still have been successful; if King Stephen faced these problems do you think King John would face similar ones; if this is how the Sioux survived the winter, what do you think they might have done in the spring?*

- **Analysis** – This requires pupils to examine, classify, categorise, research, contrast, compare, assemble, differentiate, separate, investigate and subdivide. Pupils will see patterns, be concerned over organisation of parts, recognise hidden meanings and identify components. *For example: what is the relationship between Harold's troops being tired and the change in the wind in the Channel; what are the key features of mediaeval kingship; how would you categorise the different jobs that Sioux women had to do?*

- **Synthesis** – This level of thinking requires pupils to combine information, to use old ideas to create new ones and to generalise from previous knowledge. *For example: what did Harold need to do differently to have won the Battle of Hastings; looking at all the sources, why did King John sign Magna Carta; what might be three key principles that the Sioux lead their lives by?*

- **Evaluation** – This level of thinking requires pupils to justify their ideas, assess the value of theories and presentations and make choices based on argument. *For example: do you think it would have been better if Harold had not gone north to fight Hardraada; how might you prioritise the causes of the signing of Magna Carta; why do you think other people think that the Sioux were a savage nation?*

Vygotsky's concepts

The Russian psychologist Lev Vygotsky has given us two useful concepts that help us think about challenge: a 'zone of proximal development' and 'cognitive conflict'.

A zone of proximal development

One of the key premises of Vygotsky's psychology is the notion that cognitive development is a social and cultural activity with interaction between teacher and pupil, thought and language. One of the key distinctions Vygotsky makes is that there is a difference between what pupils are able to do, know or think through by themselves and what they are only able to do with full teacher support. The gap between these two abilities is the 'zone of proximal development'. The more pupils are able to work in this area the more they will be challenged and the more they will progress. This is an important notion with some important implications. Previously we began to think about the differences between difficulty and challenge. We wondered whether in many cases teachers made tasks more **difficult** for able pupils instead of making them more **challenging**, because they made pupils work by themselves instead of in groups, gave them less time, gave them source material with a higher literacy demand without demanding higher thinking, and asked for greater precision.

However, if we are asking pupils to think harder then it might be that we actually need to give teacher support to able pupils. If they are working at the limits of their thinking then they will need teacher intervention to help them 'unblock' sticking points in aspects of their thinking, to help them through misconceptions, and to 'nudge' their thinking so that they consider other possibilities.

If we are asking able pupils to think harder then this means that they will need more time rather than less. If they are going to be thinking hard then they will probably need to do this in groups. This raises implications for how you want to group pupils in the classroom.

Careful consideration will need to be given to how material is scaffolded for able pupils. They need enough information so that they can make meaningful analyses. The more they know, the wider 'frame of reference' they have and the greater the possibility they can detect anomalies and analogies with what they know already. However, if they are swamped with information or the information is presented in too difficult a format then it can depress pupil thinking and performance.

Cognitive conflict

We have been hinting at this concept throughout this chapter. Vygotsky argued that pupils learnt the most when they were presented with information/data which challenges the learning they have achieved so far. In this instance the pupils are then required to revaluate and restructure the learning that has taken place. This means that pupils cannot treat information and learning as inert pieces of information but that knowledge is dynamic and constantly refiguring itself. A powerful way of doing this is by asking pupils to look at historical events in oblique ways via intriguing questions:

- Why didn't everybody become a Protestant?

- Two bullets and ten million deaths – how did one assassination lead to world war?

- Why did the development of anaesthetics **increase** the mortality rate in surgery?

- Is Britain more or less democratic in 2006 than it was in 1830?

So when we set tasks to able pupils we need to:

- set them activities, which require high order thinking. Bloom's taxonomy can be a useful guide

- present pupils with historical materials that help create cognitive conflict

- think about how pupil thinking can be supported by use of time, teacher intervention and literacy issues.

History and thinking skills

Few teachers cannot be aware of the work that has been done on thinking skills in the past twenty years. Yet the term itself is difficult to pin down. It can also seem strange to many history practitioners that thinking skills should be considered a discrete area – how can there be a history lesson that does not require pupil thinking?

However, thinking skills lessons do require a different emphasis. It is not that in ordinary lessons thinking does not take place but that in these lessons the nature of the **thinking becomes an explicit area for reflection**. Pupils reflect on the thinking strategies that they have used, the processes that they went through and the questions they asked and answered. Through this reflection pupils and teachers can identify misconceptions and make 'good' thinking more explicit. This explicit thinking about thinking and its refinement is known as 'metacognition'. The impact on pupil learning is this. If we think of intelligence as a malleable rather than a fixed concept then it becomes possible to 'increase' people's intelligence by making them more efficient thinkers.

There have been a wide number of commentators on thinking skills and although they differ in emphasis they have the following aspects in common:

- explicit time in the classroom for metacognition and 'bridging'

- modelling of processes to make the thinking required explicit

- learning intentions that make thinking explicit

- activities that actually require pupils to think!

The work of two theoreticians is of particular interest to us: Matthew Lipman and David Leat. Their approaches are especially useful to the history practitioner.

Matthew Lipman and 'philosophy for children'

Matthew Lipman published the second edition of his book *Thinking in Education* in 2003. In it his stated aim was to help pupils become more 'reasonable thinkers'.

> Many aspects of the world – particularly those that deal with human conduct – cannot be dealt with or formulated with the precision characteristic of science. Approximations are needed, and we have to develop a sense of the appropriate rather than expect our thought and the shape of things to correspond exactly. We must be content to reach an equitable solution, not necessarily one that is right in all the details. We must be satisfied with a sensible or reasonable outcome even if it is not strictly speaking a 'rational one'.
>
> (Lipman 2003, p. 21)

This notion of reasonableness is helpful to us. History as a subject deals with truth claims, which deal in possibilities and what is plausible, rather than what we can empirically prove or verify the same way that science can. Most of the time we do not deal with absolute certainty but we talk in terms of which possibilities are more probable than others. Having a notion of what is reasonable rather than certain can help pupils who seem to be imprisoned by the notion that their viewpoint is an 'opinion' and therefore sacred and cannot be disproved, or who seem to want to deal in the concrete and think that because one possibility does not fit the model then the model itself is inappropriate. Consider the pupils who talk in terms of bias of sources rather than viewpoint. Consider pupils who talk of truth and usefulness rather than perspective and possibility. Historical thinking requires a reasonable and almost judicial use of language. One of the trickiest essay questions that pupils have to answer is the 'To what extent' question, a question that requires balance, reasonableness and the weighing-up of factors. This is virtually impossible if pupils are thinking in terms of absolutes.

Lipman's approach to this was the 'philosophy for children' (or P4C for those in the know!). He advocated the formation of a 'community of enquiry' within the classroom. The pedagogical device for this was the use of a narrative story and then for pupils, in class, to discuss a number of philosophically based questions around it. In the main these questions would focus on motive, intent, cause, consequence and counterfactual possibility. Pupils would, through class discussion, unpick these issues and create a reasoned and reasonable dialogue. An important aspect of this process would be for pupils to consider the nature of the dialogue that was created and determine what part of this made it reasonable and what parts were less satisfactory. See Appendix 4.2 for a history example.

The work of David Leat

The work of David Leat and the University of Newcastle Thinking Skills group is another rich vein to tap into. At the time Leat was the lead PGCE Geography lecturer. In conjunction with his PGCE students he developed a number of activities that addressed the generic thinking skills that the National Curriculum requires that pupils develop. These were:

- odd one out
- concept maps
- lifelines
- mysteries
- reading photographs and pictures
- mind movies
- maps from memory
- classification
- sequencing and continuums.

This has broadened out. Newcastle University, in conjunction with Chris Kingston Publishing, have produced a series of books that have exemplified these strategies and added some others in different curriculum areas. The late Peter Fisher, with Ian Wilkinson, developed a package exemplifying those strategies in history. The following are some examples of how they might work in the history lesson.

Odd one out

This strategy is designed to make pupils think harder about concepts and their relationships and part–whole relationships. This is done by presenting pupils with a set of examples of at least two concepts – pupils have to determine which is the odd one out.

> Dictator – Secret Police – Voting – Prime Minister – Paramilitaries
> Which is the 'odd one out' and why?

In doing this particular activity pupils will be:

- drawing upon their own knowledge and understanding

- investigating possible relationships between the different pieces of information

- considering various overarching concepts that can be used to connect these pieces of information

- placing these overarching concepts into a hierarchy; to select one which provides a best fit.

They may also examine layers of meaning with the pieces of information.

When I wrote the example I had it in mind that the pupils would select 'Prime Minister' as the odd one out. The other pieces of information might be linked to the concept of totalitarianism. 'Prime Minister' is a title of an office which is usually connected to democratic countries. 'Voting' will require some reflection on the parts of pupils and will get them talking. They will want to connect it to the idea of democracy. However, with the examples they are likely to have covered, Nazi Germany and Stalinist Russia, they should know that voting took place in those countries. The fact that you could only vote for one party is a minor detail. The fact that you were expected to turn out and vote is another difference. This is a strategy that forces pupils to think in terms of analogy, anomaly, ambiguity and shades of meaning.

Concept maps

This is a tool that will be very familiar to history teachers. The idea is for pupils to determine relationships between pieces of information based around a key question. In the middle of a sheet is placed a key question or the name of a concept, e.g. *Why did Hitler become chancellor in 1933? Why did Germany invade Poland in 1939?* Or *Totalitarianism.*

Then around the central question or concepts are supporting pieces of information, e.g. *Why did Hitler become chancellor in 1933? – Treaty of Versailles, Wall Street Crash, weakness of democracy, images of power, Hitler support needed by right-wing groups.*

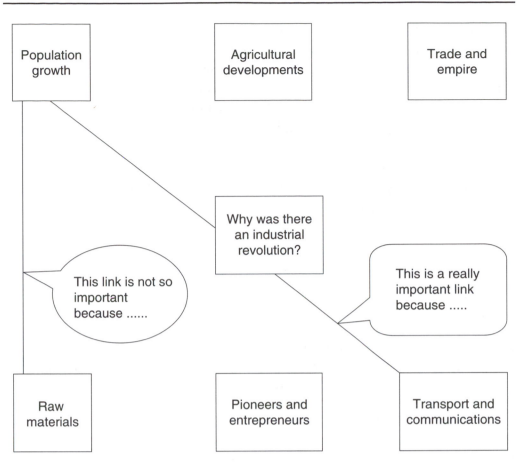

Concept map example

Pupils are then required, in groups, to draw connecting lines between different pieces of information and the central concept and question. They annotate these lines to explain what the relationship is. They can, if asked, colour code the different connections, with highlighter pens, to represent, for example, economic, social, political connections: green if they think the connections are really important, yellow if in the middle and red if they think it is not an important connection. Using the same principles can they identify connections which represent long term/short term causes and trends? Can they identify those connections which are necessary/sufficient/direct/indirect? Can they add their own extra pieces of information? How might this activity help support pupil writing?

Lifelines

Teachers are used to presenting information to pupils graphically. In this activity pupils are presented with a graph. The bottom axis is time. The vertical axis represents a continuum and there is a midpoint which represents a neutral zone. The continuum is between positive and negative or happy and sad. Pupils are given an information set on card. They then have to plot the information on the graph. This enables them to analyse a process and determine its ups and downs.

Mysteries

This is one of the most successful and exciting strategies that Leat and his associates have developed. The idea behind it is that pupils are given a problem to solve that is best expressed in personal terms and suggests a mystery, problem or tension to solve. They are then given about 20–30 pieces of information on card and then asked to solve the mystery. Some pieces of information are confusing, ambiguous and irrelevant. Some cards will only be useful when inferences are made from them. Different solutions are possible, but pupils should be able to arrive at a probable or a set of probable answers. There will definitely be multiple routes into reaching an answer. One of the most valuable parts of this lesson is the metacognitive debrief where pupils are asked to reflect upon the route they took, which questions, decisions and pieces of information helped them and which were a hindrance. This is an activity that works really well because:

- the element of mystery acts as a hook

- phrasing the mystery in personal terms intrigue children and makes the mystery more concrete and accessible

- pupils work in groups. Thus the group can draw upon collaborative rather than individual thinking. There is also a greater capacity with the group to handle larger amounts of information than an individual pupil

- there is genuine challenge.

An example of a mystery can be seen in Appendix 4.3.

Reading photographs and pictures

We have long known the importance of the visual element in history and that pictorial sources can be more accessible for less literate learners. We also know that pupils in their ordinary everyday culture are being exposed to more visual stimulation and less literary stimulants then ever before.

Pupils are increasingly able to generate increasingly sophisticated understandings from visual sources. In order for this activity to work well it is important that:

- pupils analyse the pictures in depth and that they develop specific tools to do so

- pupils are able to place the visual sources into a wider historical context

- pupils deconstruct and analyse the pictures as part of a process of enquiry

- pupils use the pictures to speculate and hypothesise.

A useful tool can be to ask the pupils to examine the picture as a whole, then split the pictures into quadrants and examine it. Then ask them to consider the picture as a whole again and check whether their initial thinking has changed.

Pupils could also use a variation of a 'layers of inference' diagram. The picture is placed in the centre of a set of concentric rectangles. The next rectangle outside of the picture invites pupils to write down what they can see in the

What other questions do I need to ask?

What doesn't the source tell me?

What guesses can I make – what can I infer?

What does the source definitely tell me?

PEACE AND FUTURE CANNON FODDER

The Tiger: "Curious! I seem to hear a child weeping!"

Layers of inference diagram, showing 'Peace and Future Cannon Fodder' cartoon

picture. The next rectangle asks them to speculate what they would see if the scope of the picture was enlarged. The next rectangle asks them to speculate about what they thought happened before the picture was taken. The next rectangle asks them to speculate on what will happen after the picture has been taken. The last rectangle asks them to think about how examining this picture has helped them answer their enquiry question.

Mind movies

This is a thinking strategy that asks pupils to speculate and hypothesise. It can demand that pupils draw upon previous learning and assumptions that they have. It is particularly useful for visual learners. For this activity to work pupils have to be put into a calmed and relaxed state (!). They should stand and close their eyes. The teacher then tells them part of a story or reads them some stimulus material. However, the material is incomplete. After the teacher stops the pupils use their 'mind's eye' to complete the rest of the story. They might be encouraged to think about what they might see, hear, smell, touch and taste. They will feel very self-conscious the first time that they do this but it can be very effective. An alternative way to do this is as a parachute jump.

> Imagine that you are going to make a parachute jump from an aircraft. I want you to imagine that you are putting your parachute on and then boarding it. Now the aircraft is taking off and climbing high. This is a special aircraft because as we go higher we are also going back in time. We have now gone back to the year 1845 and we are now high over a big Victorian industrial town. Now I want you to stand up, step out of the aircraft and begin your descent. As you drift down towards the town what can you see, what can you hear, what can you taste and smell? Where do you think you will land? . . . As you drift closer to the town how does your image of it change? . . . Now that you are nearly there soak up as many things as you can sense. You've landed. What do you sense now?

The teacher can now take feedback from the group about what they have seen and detected with their other senses. This makes an excellent starter and pupils can review this speculative learning at the end of a lesson as a plenary. What things were they 'right' about; what misconceptions did they have; what things are they unsure about and will need investigating in the next lesson?

Maps from memory

This is an excellent way of getting pupils to process large amounts of information or big picture learning in a collaborative way. In its simplest form there is a piece of information on paper in front of the teacher. The pupils are put into groups. A relay race follows as pupils send one person at a time from their group up to the information, examine it, then return to their group and reproduce what they have seen. Originally Leat used this with pupils to replicate maps, however we can use this strategy in a number of ways:

- maps of famous historical events, battles, historical cities etc.

- pictures of historical interest – cartoons, illustrations etc.

- spider diagrams of key structures of information, e.g. a set of images and text which show the road to war between 1919 and 1939.

With the spider diagrams it can be useful sometimes if the 'arms' of the spider are not in the correct order and pupils are invited to sequence them.

Classification

This activity requires pupils to examine a large amount of information and then classify it into different groups. The teacher could supply the headings or the pupils could generate their own headings depending upon the ability of the pupils and the complexity of the material. If the headings are generated by the group this is an excellent way for pupils to generate a set of key features for a historical period.

Sequencing and continuums

Another way of using cards is simply to give pupils data sets of information and ask them to sequence it into chronological order by looking for cause and effect. We can ask pupils to place pieces of information on a continuum. For example, one difficulty that many pupils have is to make inferences from source material **and** think about the degree of possibility and probability of that inference. Instead why not give the pupils the source and the inferences that can be made on individual pieces of card. Then give the pupils a continuum where the categories are 'true, probably true, possibly true, ambiguous, possibly not true, probably not true and false'. Working in groups pupils have to determine the best place for the individual statements and work towards an understanding of the rationale behind what makes an inference probable, possible, uncertain or less likely to be true.

History and creativity

Before we examine how we might use creative thinking within history it is best to specify what creative thinking is not. This is really important because, as we saw in Chapter 3 (identification), creativity is a key way of identifying the able child and we must make provision for this, but creativity suffers from people holding a number of misconceptions regarding it:

- Creativity is simply a spontaneous way of thinking that comes from within – it cannot be 'taught' or nurtured.

- Creativity is simply based around activity rather than thinking.

- Creativity is allowing the pupils to simply produce creative things – pictures, drama or singing.

The National Advisory Committee on Creative and Cultural Education (NACCCE) published a report in 1999 called *All Our Futures: Creativity, Culture and Education* that took a more helpful view of creativity. Here it defined creativity as follows:

> Creativity is not simply a matter of letting go. Serious creative achievement relies on knowledge, control of materials, and command of ideas. Creative education involves a balance between teaching knowledge and skills, and encouraging innovation.

and:

Imaginative activity is a form of mental play – serious play directed towards some creative purpose. It is a mode of thought which is essentially generative: in which we attempt to expand the possibilities of a given situation; to look at it afresh from a new perspective, encouraging alternatives to the routine or expected in any given task ... Creative insights often occur when existing ideas are combined to reinterpret in unexpected ways or when they are applied in areas in which they are not normally associated. Often this arises by making unusual connections, seeing analogies and relationships between ideas or objects that have not previously been related.

Some of the implications for this mean that creativity is grounded in firm historical understanding. Genuine creative learning takes place when pupils are asked to examine their understanding in an unusual way. The key to this is using the unusual. We must be aware of the dangers of being stuck in the same groove and thinking it is creativity. Newspaper front pages, speeches and even some role-playing activities have become a little worn. What we want are pupils to look at their historical understanding from a genuinely unusual perspective to generate insights and new understandings that would not normally be available to them.

Synetics and metaphorical understanding

A way of achieving this is through the model of learning called synetics. In the book *Models of Learning – Tools for Teaching* by Joyce, Calhoun and Hopkins (2002), the authors put forward a number of different models of lessons that can be used for pupil learning. The model for learning they called synetics was to develop pupil understanding by the creative generation of metaphors. The lesson model is structured like this:

1. description of the present situation

2. direct analogies

3. personal analogies

4. compressed conflict

5. re-examination of the original student task.

Description of the present situation

Year 8 pupils were working on an evaluation of the life of Oliver Cromwell. They were doing pretty well at recounting many of the key events of his life, but their understandings of his life were limited. The words they used were simple things like good or bad, tragic and cruel, etc. They also had a tendency to polarise phases within his life as 'for the king', 'republican' and 'warlike'. Their responses were predictable, pedestrian and lacked feeling and insight. To counter this the teacher decided to generate a set of metaphorical understandings.

Direct analogies

The next phase was to ask for pupils to make a direct analogy between the area of study and something **completely** disassociated with it. The teacher asked them for a series of **big cats** that they might associate with Oliver Cromwell. Responses might include lion, panther, tiger, cheetah and leopard. At this point there was a tendency to make direct comparisons and metaphors between the object of study – Cromwell – and the substance for the direct analogy, e.g. thinking of Cromwell's consistency and the leopard, the speed he reacted to events with the cheetah, the image of the evil Shere Khan in the Disney film of the *Jungle Book* and the power of the panther. However, the teacher did not want to draw out the analogies too much yet as the teacher wanted to take a moment to compare a personal analogy.

Personal analogy

At this stage the teacher asked the pupils to **select one direct analogy** that seemed to be the **furthest away** from the object of study. The pupils selected the panther. The teacher then asked them to think of the world from the perspective of the panther, how would a panther think and feel? The pupils responded in a number of ways. They said the panther might feel 'irritable and hungry', 'prowling and powerful', 'blinkered and not able to see', 'deliberate in its movements', 'slow, but ready to strike', 'always ready to strike', 'always hungry', 'powerful, but weak and vulnerable', 'a planner and a stalker'.

Compressed conflict

The teacher then took some of these personal analogies and juxtaposed dichotomous statements, such as 'deliberate hunger', 'powerfully vulnerable' and 'a blinkered stalker'. The pupils then, from a more extensive list, selected the ones they liked the best.

Re-examination of the original task

The teacher then asked the pupils how these new metaphors could be used to generate further understandings of the life of Cromwell.

- How appropriate do you think is the term 'deliberate hunger'? *Pupils pondered whether this might mean that he had a plan to get rid of the king, were his steps always deliberate and considered, what was his hunger – a desire for power, his perception of duty to God? Did the term 'deliberate hunger' mean that he kept himself pure and zealous – how could the term be used?*

- How appropriate do you think is the term 'powerfully vulnerable'? *Pupils pondered in what ways was Cromwell powerful, did it mean his charisma, his military background, his military ability, the power he had as Lord Protector? In what ways was he vulnerable – why did the Rule of the Saints not work – why didn't England become stable after 1649, how could such a powerful man be so isolated by 1651?*

- How appropriate do you think is the term 'blinkered stalker'? *Pupils pondered how Cromwell might have been a stalker – what did he stalk, what were his ultimate goals, do stalkers in the jungle go directly towards their prey or do they camouflage themselves and move tangentially, how and when do they pounce; was the king metaphorically not looking and vulnerable, was he, metaphorically, the weakest in the herd? How can a stalker successfully stalk if he is blinkered, did Cromwell suffer from tunnel vision, could he only see one thing in front of him, was he oblivious to circumstance?*

The metaphors generated discussions and insights into Cromwell's character that were not present before. Pupils began to articulate in increasingly sophisticated ways that moved beyond crude stereotypes and really got them thinking about Cromwell's character, motives and intentions. This kind of really sophisticated creative thinking is an excellent strategy for challenging the able child as it forces them to think from oblique angles, with sophistication, precision and qualification.

Counterfactual arguments

Counterfactual reasoning can be very helpful to pupils in helping them to determine the significance and importance of events by speculating on the consequences if they had not happened. Paradoxically to fully think and speculate in this way requires pupils to have a reasonably large amount of knowledge to draw upon. It is possibly more difficult to think well in this way rather than connecting existing patterns of causation. Although works such as Niall Ferguson's *Virtual History* (2003) have popularised it, it is Geoffrey Hawthorn's *Plausible Worlds* (1991) which has given it a more recent philosophical base.

A classroom approach that could work would be to provide pupils with a set of sequenced cards. Each card represents one key event in a crucial period. The class are then asked to subtract one of the cards from the sequence. They then have to rank the remaining cards by placing them into the following categories: *no change; hardly any change; some change; lots of change* and then explain their answers.

A second approach might be after pupils have done some work on a particular historical issue to present them with a different historical outcome to the one that actually happened, for example, German troops withdrawing from Poland in September 1939 or a rapprochement between Charles I and Parliament in 1649, and asking pupils what they think might have been necessary for this alternative to have happened. It might also be useful to ask them what they think might have happened next.

To ensure that these kinds of activities and thinking do not become frivolous it is necessary to track pupils back to historical reality. The objective of these activities is to help pupils think harder about the significance of events. Historians ascribe significance and importance to events – this is one approach to it.

What might have happened if . . . Archduke Franz Ferdinand had survived the Sarajevo Assassination?		
No change	Schlieffen Plan	War in 1914
Hardly any change	Alliance System	Germany signing the 'blank cheque' of support to Austria
Some change	Naval race	Austrian ultimatum to Serbia
Lots of change	Balkan wars	Germany invading Belgium
	Franco–Prussian war	Versailles Treaty 1919
	Outbreak of Second World war in 1939	Rise of Adolf Hitler
	Russian declaration of war on Austria–Hungary	Break-up of the Austrian–Hungarian Empire

Counterfactual reasoning example

Potential pitfalls

However, there are three potential pitfalls that need to be addressed:

- the pitfall of a **deterministic** approach. There is the danger that pupils will approach this kind of thinking in a simplistic way. They will begin to build up the notion that earlier/long term causes are the most important because they created a situation that meant that whatever short term causes there were the event would have happened anyway. This kind of thinking will be familiar to anyone who has taught an SHP developmental study.

- the pitfall of **extremity of language and thinking**. Pupils are used to thinking in extremes. They will be less likely to think about the graded significance of events or the degree of change and more likely to be thinking in terms of substitution. If one event is subtracted then the series of events are completely changed. They will be using 'either/or' language rather than increments and nuance.

- the pitfall of **post hoc** arguments. Another pitfall is that this kind of thinking **might** reinforce the misconception of events causing each other in a sequence – in other words that simply because an event preceded another that it caused what came later.

Mr Taylor again!

What do you think the impact on pupil learning might have been now for the entire class, and specifically the able child within the class, if your observation notes on Mr Taylor's lesson had read:

0920 – (DEVELOPMENT) Mr Taylor introduced the class to the notion of a sequencing activity. The pupils were put into groups and given a selection of cards. Each card recorded an event but had no date mentioned on it. Purely from the logic of the cards they were asked to sequence them. Lower ability pupils required a scaffold to help them. Principally they were told by the teacher which were the cards that formed the beginning, middle and end. The language in these cards was simpler and more leading. The ablest pupils were given no such scaffold and made to think harder. They were forced to rely more upon the logic of historical events rather than sequential language on the cards.

Plenaries and endings

There is nothing so unsatisfying as a lesson ending with the bell ringing and the teacher telling pupils to pack away their work and copy the homework off the board.

A good plenary should transform a lesson from one where pupils have been busy or engaged to one where the significance of that engagement is understood and translated into learning.

Difficulties with plenaries

However, plenaries are notoriously difficult to manage and do successfully. There are a number of reasons for this:

1. Plenaries are not allocated sufficient time in the lesson.

2. Plenaries are exclusively activity-based. This is not to say that a plenary cannot involve an activity, but rather a plenary becomes defined as an activity at the end of the lesson.

3. The teacher consolidates the learning at the end of the lesson. A plenary will not function well if the teacher **tells** the pupils what it is they have learnt.

4. There is a tendency to treat learning as a sequence and look for completeness before the next episode of the lesson is begun. Consequently the starter activity can last far too long as the teacher is reluctant to guillotine an activity before the pupils have teased out all possibilities or reached the right answer. The midpoint lasts too long because pupil activity slows or the pupils are focused on task completion. There is the failure to remember that a plenary can be a taking stock exercise in the mid-part of a wider sequence of learning.

Plenaries **are**:

1. discrete episodes in a lesson where the mode of pupil thinking changes

2. possibly slower in pace than the rest of the lesson

3. sacrosanct times for pupils to articulate their learning.

A successful plenary invites pupils to switch their thinking from an acquisition mode into a reflective one. Pupils are required to reflect because the teacher frames the plenary around one or more of the following overlapping questions:

- What have you learnt?

- How did you learn it?

- Where else might you be able to use it?

- How are you going to remember what it is you have learnt?

The first question could invite a list from pupils of everything that has been covered in the lesson, and indeed that is the usual response when the teacher first introduces these episodes. However, what this question is really demanding from the children is for them to distil and refine what they have learnt. Can they distinguish between different levels of knowledge – key points, principle examples to support key points and illustrative material? Can they make generalisations from what they have learnt? Can they place their learning in a wider context? Can they consider the implications of what it is they have learnt?

The second question requires a more sophisticated response – but it can pay real dividends for pupils. It requires that the pupils can put together the fragments of understanding they have and to put them into discrete steps or stages. It may be that the class generates the process that in a sequencing exercise they will look at the big picture first. In other words they will look at all the information and see if they can pick out a shape or overarching set of themes. Can they then select which pieces of information go at the beginning, which at the middle and which at the end? Once they have pieced together some sensible fragments can they put together the rest of the sequence? Can they check their answers at the end to determine if this is the best sequence that can be used?

The third question relates to application and bridging. We know that pupils are notoriously bad at transferring their learning from one context to another. This kind of questioning and activity tries to build up the chances of pupils seeing the connections between the different historical skills and content and other subjects.

The last question is a recognition that pupils are required to learn a good deal of historical knowledge with which to substantiate their understandings. Yet very often we do not ask pupils to explicitly think about how to remember what they have learnt – until it is revision time at the end of Year 11 and we ask them to revise everything in one go. Can pupils draw upon the use of mnemonics, mind maps, acrostics, learning journeys etc.? Not only could pupils draw upon a repertoire of strategies but they could decide which ones were the best for them.

What do you think the impact on pupil learning might have been now for the entire class, and specifically the able child within the class, if your observation notes on Mr Taylor's lesson had read:

0945 (PLENARY AND ENDINGS) – Mr Taylor calls the class together and asks them to reflect carefully on what they have learnt this lesson. He asks them to think if there are some generalisations or important conclusions they can reach. He asks them to write five things they have learnt in the back of their book, in silence. He then asks them to snowball their answers by first working in pairs and then in fours. When they have compared answers he asks them to choose what they think are the five most important things they have learnt. After a few moments he takes some feedback from individual groups, using the questioning techniques described earlier in this chapter; the rest of the class evaluate and comment on them. He then asks the groups how they will remember the five pieces of information they have identified. Some use mnemonics and some opt for visual recording. Mr Taylor mutters something about Hitler's actions being consistent with traditional German foreign policy and then asks the pupils to pack their books away.

The earlier part of the chapter describes how different parts of a lesson can be changed to make it more cognitively challenging. The next part of this chapter describes how certain themes can be developed over a sequence of lessons.

Building independent learning

It is sometimes assumed that the capacity to be independent is a characteristic of the more able learner. This is not the case. It is possible to see less able pupils go off and work independently on a project and able pupils look confused over the notion of private study. The capacity to be an independent learner is something which has to be built up and planned for by the teacher.

To be independent as a learner there are at least two important constituent parts. The first are a set of enquiry and information processing skills. These might include:

- the ability to select, frame and pose genuine historical questions

- the ability to plan work to a given timeframe and deadline

- the knowledge of how to search for, collate and sift through sources of information

- literacy demands – reading for purpose and at speed, note taking and various styles of writing.

The second set of skills relates to certain modes of learning and thinking:

- the ability to determine what you are learning rather than what you are doing and how the two bits might interconnect

- the ability to sequence and structure information

- the ability to determine cause and consequence

- the ability to deconstruct and reconstruct from historical sources.

In other words we want pupils to be able to think historically. This will not happen if pupils are simply presented with a set of projects or activities and then asked to complete them. Pupils will become independent learners when:

- teachers plan for the historical learning that they want pupils to engage in

- pupils are explicitly aware of this

- the teacher helps the pupils build up a set of discrete and independent learning strategies through a mixture of modelling and metacognitive debriefs.

In other words the lessons that the pupils have look more like Mr Taylor's second lesson than the first.

Opportunities for independent learning

If pupils are to be given an opportunity for independent learning or historical enquiry then the following components should be seen as useful.

Enquiry guides

An enquiry guide could include:

- an overarching historical question

- a guide on how to set secondary questions that help answer the overarching question

- success criteria that give the pupils an idea of what good might look like

- a list of easily accessible resources and hints on how to find others

- pupil choice over outcomes. Will the work be presented in project form, as a web page, tape recording or video etc?

- pupil outcomes could be linked to multiple intelligences. Howard Gardner suggests that there are multiple entry points to subject material: collaborative, existential, narrative, hands on, aesthetic, logical–quantitative and intrapersonal. So a piece of independent work on the Holocaust might require pupils to: work together independently in a small group and present a set of discussion papers (**collaborative**); consider what a study of the Holocaust might reveal about human nature (**existential**); consider the Holocaust as a story or narrative (**narrative**); consider the Holocaust by performing a role play, producing maps, videos etc. (**hands on**); consider the nature of the Holocaust from statistical data (**logical–quantitative**); and produce a piece of work by themselves (**intrapersonal**.) Of course in real life pupils will draw upon all those areas but it might be a teacher's job to ensure that they can do this.

The author remembers fondly an able Year 9 group that he taught in his NQT year. They had worked for a term on the Royal Navy at the time of Nelson. To conclude this piece of work they had to complete a project from a selection of questions on naval life and the biography of Nelson. One pupil went into the crypt of Rochester Cathedral to record the funeral service of Nelson and interviews with his contemporaries. Another wrote the biography as an interview with Bob Henries, Nelson's fictional faithful boatswain. My favourite was the pupil who reproduced, in an 'authentic' box, her correspondence between Nelson and Lady Hamilton. It is possible to argue that these things tend to focus pupils' attention onto presentation rather than learning, but the author's view is what the hell!

Learning log

A second strategy is to have a learning log, which is at least read by the teacher and handed in by the pupil as a project component even if it is not formally marked. This should be a diary that outlines the processes and difficulties that the pupils went through. It is worth spending a lesson using these diaries as a resource as they provide the metacognitive bit for the class. How did they sequence their project and research? What went well and what was more of a challenge and what will they do differently next time?

Formative assessment strategies – assessment for learning

It is beyond the scope of this chapter to describe in detail how assessment for learning in history might work. However it is an important aspect of pedagogy to reflect upon. The work of Paul Black and Dylan Williams is seminal and *Inside the Black Box* (1998) is required reading. The key messages from it seem to be:

- Assessment is a key tool in the teacher's armoury to raise pupil achievement.

- For assessment to be effective a dialogue needs to be established between teacher–pupil and their learning.

- Pupils and teachers need to establish where pupils are, where they need to be and how to close the gap.

- This needs to be done by a process of reflection rather than compliance. How can a piece of work be improved rather than if I do this I might get an extra mark?

- The excessive use of grades and rankings of pupils produces a negative performance orientated culture rather than a learning/mastery culture.

In a lesson this might be achieved by the use of:

1. learning objectives – to clarify what is being learnt.

2. learning outcomes – to state what pupils will produce.

3. a discussion of the relationship between points 1 and 2.

4. success criteria. **This is not the same as a mark scheme** – much less a set of level descriptors in pupil speak. A mark scheme is a graded set of levels of

response. For example, in an essay mark scheme we might move from simple description to detailed description; from detailed description to simple explanation; from simple explanation to analysis. Each band might have a caricature or set of characteristics and 3–5 available marks. This kind of thing will be very familiar to anybody who has marked at GCSE. Success criteria are much more focused and will identify those characteristics that make a particular outcome good. For example, in an essay that deals with causation there might be success criteria that focus pupils on explanatory language; the use of pithy topic sentences; the importance of pee-ing (*point, explanation, evidence*); and making a final judgement. Even better are those success criteria that cannot be used as checklists. They can be accessed by all but require effort and thought to translate them into the outcome, e.g. points are backed by appropriate examples (*pupils will need to discuss what we mean by appropriate*); pupils will need to show strong relationships between the causes (*what is a strong relationship and how does it differ from a link between the causes?*); pupils will need to explain why people argue over which causes are the most significant (*this certainly takes pupil thinking onto a higher level*); pupils need to use clear language that conveys their meaning (*what do we mean by clear – is this the same as saying that the longest answer is the best or the one with the longest words is better?*).

5. teachers exemplifying what a good outcome looks like. This may be in the form of teacher- or pupil-produced examples that pupils can deconstruct or by the teacher modelling the process to make explicit positive steps and potential pitfalls.

6. opportunities for pupil–peer and self-assessment. A lot of peer- and self-assessment that takes place in schools is geared towards generating targets and reflection over learning that has taken place over a considerable period of time. We can find plenty of end of unit reflection sheets and forms where it is not unusual to find that pupils promise faithfully to work harder, pay more attention, stop talking to their friends and get a higher grade at the next test. We may take a cynical view of this. In this scenario pupils are being asked to assess too much over too long a period of time. Pupils can set themselves a target that will vary depending upon whether it is for a Key Stage or GCSE qualification, what they will do in a term, a week or in the remaining 15 minutes of the lesson. The shorter the time limit the more focused and productive the target is likely to be. In essence pupils work best when they can reflect upon and identify what they need to do to improve the quality of a particular outcome.

7. a reflective plenary that allows pupils to identify next steps and the strengths and weakness of their learning. It should allow the teacher to do the same and inform short term planning.

The impact of this should be to raise the overall **achievement** of pupils by one Key Stage level or GCSE grade with the biggest impact on the lower attaining pupils. However, for the more able pupil it allows the teacher to encourage and teach pupils to be more independent and acquire higher order learning skills. It should prepare able pupils better for the requirements of AS/A2 study and GCSE coursework. Of even more significance if the 14–19 curriculum qualifications start to specify that to gain the higher grades pupils need to get good outcomes independently, then this is a process that will help able pupils acquire that independence. *Teaching History 115 – Assessment Without Levels?* (June 2004) is an excellent place to start looking for historical examples, especially the articles by Sally Burnham and Geraint Brown, and Mark Cottingham and Simon Butler. The Key Stage 3 National Strategy Assessment for Learning whole school training materials has subject exemplification for history and a set of INSET tasks. These may be used with profit. Appendix 4.4 provides an example of how a lesson structure that is rich in formative assessment strategies might look.

In many senses this has been a difficult chapter to write. Traditionally there has been a tendency to make various assumptions about able pupils. Firstly that an able pupil is an independent learner. This is not true. Secondly that an able pupil is a literate learner. Not true. Thirdly that an able pupil will have an explicit set of learning strategies at their disposal. Not true. Fourthly that simply by looking at more complex sources and dealing with more information able pupils will be catered for. Not true. The last point may be a way of allowing teachers, in conjunction with other strategies, of making more complex demands on pupils, but by itself it is not enough. This has meant that any consideration of teaching the able has meant considering what we might mean by good teaching and learning full stop. This chapter is not a definitive answer by any means, but hopefully it has given the reader an appetite to consider what makes good learning in their own particular school, to consider the impact on pupils of any given teaching strategy and to consider what they think the needs are of their able pupils and how they might be begun to be met.

CHAPTER 5

Support for learning

- Support for different SEN pupils
- The role of learning mentors and the SENCO
- The use of the school library
- Links with parents

In Chapter 3 we identified able pupils by using two criteria – their visible abilities now and the potential they might have to achieve well in the future. In this chapter we shift our thinking again by considering them as a group of pupils with particular sets of needs. We shall consider the needs of able pupils who have other special educational needs. Then, in a more general sense, we shall examine the needs of more able pupils and how they can be supported outside of the classroom.

Pupils with other special educational needs

There are two main issues with these children. The first is an **identification issue** – that people will not see beyond their special needs and not think of them as possibly being able. The second is the selection of **appropriate strategies** that can be used to help the individual pupil with their special needs and make them better historians.

Pupils with special educational needs vary in their needs, for example:

- Autism spectrum – pupils may show great talents in specific areas, e.g. art or maths.

- Specific learning difficulties/dyslexia – pupils' ability may be obscured by poor literacy skills. Such pupils are likely to experience a low self-esteem and considerable frustration. A real issue for teachers is that a 'common sense' indicator of ability in history is that pupils have high levels of literacy. These pupils are at risk of 'slipping the net' as their ability to reason and think is hidden by their poor writing skills. Recognition of particular strengths is very important in raising self-esteem and peer credibility.

- Physical difficulties, e.g. cerebral palsy, and associated difficulties may be so encompassing that an agile mind can sometimes become underchallenged. Careful learning assessment over time is particularly important for pupils with physical difficulties.

- Sensory impairments such as hearing loss or vision impairment do not themselves limit the ability to think, but there will need to be an opportunity to change and adopt an appropriate medium.

- Emotional and behavioural difficulties often mask a pupil's true potential. This is particularly the case of pupils who have not been identified as gifted or talented and so may feel frustrated and experience low self-esteem. We have also indicated that an important element of learning is the ability to communicate and collaborate. This learning skill may be masked and teacher expectations of the pupil depressed.

We shall discuss the nature of some of these needs in this chapter and suggest some approaches, general and subject-specific, to tackle them.

Autism spectrum

The autism spectrum describes three related and interlocking conditions – classic autism, Asperger syndrome and Semantic Pragmatic disorder. The rate of incidence of these conditions vary. For example, autism has an incidence of 4–5 cases per 10,000 births. Asperger syndrome has a rate of 36 cases per 10,000 births. In general the gender ratio of incidence is four boys for every girl.

All three conditions are characterised by these impairments:

- inability to relate and interact with others

- inability to communicate socially

- lack of imagination and repetitive behaviour. Children on the autism spectrum take things very literally and have difficulty with analogy, metaphor, rhetoric, irony and sarcasm.

Children with classic autism will also tend to:

- be aloof and distant from others – pre-occupied in their own world

- have abnormal speech and language patterns. Apart from developing language skills comparatively late in life their speech may be confused, difficult to utter, full of semantic and grammatical errors, very concrete and real, and have phonological and severe mispronunciations.

In addition they may have motor abnormality – such as repetitive banging of the head or swaying. There may be intellectual subnormality. There may be compulsive repetitive behaviour and rituals.

This presents the teacher of history with a number of challenges, not least because history uses language in a particular way. We use language in an essentially abstract way to discuss abstract events. It may be possible to model concrete procedures and skills. It may be possible to show concrete examples of outcomes that pupils will produce, but history deals with the past, what has been rather than what is reproducible here and now like a science laboratory or a design and technology workshop.

Autistic pupils benefit from the following:

- clearly defined structure and routine

- concrete examples of reality and processing – modelling

- visual entry points into materials – such as artistry or computer work

- the minimising of aural and visual interference. Background noise can play havoc – humming or the noise of a radiator

- reading and writing can be difficult – especially if seen from a different, empathetic, perspective – typing is certainly easier

- these pupils are uni-channel – they tend to only be able to use one sensory perception at a time – do not ask for more than this

- advanced organisers can be really useful – they find remembering more than the immediate to be very difficult. Knowledge tends to be locked in a specific context.

Asperger syndrome is one of a range of autism-like disorders which often manifests in 'eccentric' behaviour rather than obvious disability. At one time Asperger syndrome was perceived as high functioning autism but this is now under question and may be more properly considered as a disorder in its own right. These pupils are more likely to be defined as able. They may have excellent memory and vocabulary skills, but it may be possible that comprehension and understanding is more limited. They have problems dealing with the abstract rather than the concrete. They can be strong visual thinkers, but still they will be thinking in a literal way. They will find social relationships and collaboration difficult and will find that they have their own interests. They will exemplify the 'goofy gifted' kid. These are the pupils who will tell you everything you wanted to know, and stuff that you did not know, about the Tiger Tank and the German Army on the Eastern Front, 1941–5, but will be unable to handle abstract notions of causation.

Strategies for teachers

The following ideas may be helpful when you plan your lessons:

- Call the pupil by name before addressing the class or they may not know you are talking to them.

- Use lots of visual support materials. Back up oral instructions with writing or drawings. The use of advanced organisers and visual stimulus material can be crucial here.

- Vary questioning style. Include concrete questions and then move to the abstract.

- Sitting may be a problem. If they have dyspraxic tendencies they may prefer to stand. Point out pupils who are already sitting to help clarify instruction.

- Avoid eye contact or direct attention.

- Take an interest in what they know about and let them share it with the class.

- Let them make things – models, games, cartoons.

- Encourage the use of non-competitive games, such as taking turns or loop cards.

- Keep to a classroom routine. Print up a checklist.

- Use story boards with identified sentences and language in a common format – describe, perspective, directive and control.

- Use talking frames for classroom discussion and group work.

- Model everything and then model it again.

Case study: Malcolm, Year 7 (Asperger syndrome)

In spite of careful liaison between the primary school and the head of Year 7, teachers were still taken by surprise when they met Malcolm. They had not appreciated that he would have to be taught many things that other children pick up by observation. For instance, he did not understand about queuing for his lunch and simply crawled between everyone's legs to get to the food.

His speech is robotic and it can be disconcerting when he does not give the expected answer but simply says whatever is in his head at the time. He does not understand tact and might say 'That dress is old', without appreciating that this could give offence. Sometimes he becomes obsessed by a door or window and wants it opened to a particular angle. This same obsession is apparent in his written work where he can become anxious if teachers try to persuade him to set it out in a different way.

He is a very able mathematician and should reach university level in three or four years. However, he cannot cope with group work or group investigations and will become quite agitated if put into such a situation. Malcolm is also an outstanding chess player and was representing the school within a few weeks of arriving. In all other academic subjects he copes quite well in the top set although his very literal understanding of some concepts can create problems, particularly in English.

Sport is a mystery to him. He does not understand the rules and is, in any case, lumbering and ungainly. It is during these lessons that his peers are most likely to be unkind, although, on the whole, they are quite protective towards him.

Strategies

- Coordinate support for Malcolm across the school. One person should be responsible for monitoring him on a regular basis and dealing with any recurrent problems.

- Teach any social skills he lacks in a very simple and direct way. For example, when someone says 'How are you?' you say, 'Fine, thank you.'

- Where Malcolm finds group work distressing, he could work as one of a pair, in which he has a specific task to accomplish that does not demand long periods of interaction.

- Encourage other pupils to be proud of his achievements for the school when he plays in the chess team.

- Try to use as many visual sources as you can with him.

- His main strength seems to be logical–mathematical intelligence. Therefore sequencing events, providing him with rules to follow in identifying cause and dealing with source material will help. Try to present historical information to him qualitatively. Routines and procedures will be important – the craft and art side of things can be developed later.

- The use of ICT can be very helpful. Try using, in a mediated way, the Learning Curve website or the British Library Source CDs.

Dyslexia

The definition of dyslexia used by the Dyslexia Institute is as follows:

Dyslexia causes difficulties in learning to read, write and spell. Short-term memory, maths, concentration, personal organisation and sequencing may also be affected. It arises from a weakness in the processing of language-based information.

The research protocol for identifying learners who are dyslexic is that their reading and writing abilities should be two years below their chronological age. The DfES criteria states that they should be in the bottom 20% of reading and writing. The problem is that able children tend to have very good memories. This means that it is likely that their ability to read is not too severely impaired.

The chances are that they will have learnt to read by rote. The kind of pupil we are describing here is one who has an adequate reading age but who finds it incredibly difficult to write. It is likely that they will have tried to mask and hide their difficulties. They might be good at ICT, sport, cartoons and diagrammatic communication. They will have the most difficulty when they are required to both process information and communicate it at the same time, e.g. responding in a lecture, taking notes, writing under timed conditions, writing up notes on new information in class. As already implied, if the pupils have been successful in masking their disability then another problem might be lack of teacher awareness of the issues. They might describe pupils as lazy, slapdash, scruffy and lacking attention to detail.

Strategies for teachers
Use the following to help plan your lessons:

- Provide intervention on misspellings of crucial words – mnemonics for instance or rules such as 'i before e except after c'.

- Divide a unit of work into lesson sequences. Some lessons should focus on gaining historical understanding – some lessons should focus on communicating those understandings.

- Use any writing strategy advocated by Christine Counsell – see especially *History and Literacy in Year 7* (2004).

- Use talk and thinking skills strategies first, such as the use of cognitively challenging questions and the strategies described in Chapter 4. These strategies and the use of collaborative work will provide a way for pupils to think their way through material without grappling with the writing at the same time. This will provide a plank for the literacy strategies that can be used later on.

- Provide a scaffold for pupils – the use of study guides which contain key pieces of information, writing and sorting frames to aid communication.

- These strategies will not only aid dyslexics.

Case study: Michael, Year 9 (dyslexic)

Michael obtained a place at a boys' grammar school but has struggled ever since. He has an extensive vocabulary and always volunteers for drama productions and reporting back when working in a group. He enjoys music, art and DT and brings a keen imagination and wit to all these subjects. Michael prefers the company of teachers and older pupils with whom he likes to debate topical issues. His peers, on the other hand, regard him as a 'bit of a wimp' as he does not enjoy sport and frequently corrects their behaviour.

After a very slow start in early childhood, Michael can now read fluently but his other problems associated with dyslexia remain. His spelling and handwriting are very poor. He finds it almost impossible to obtain information from large swathes of text. Even when the main ideas are summarised for him in bullet points, he still has difficulty revising for examinations or tests or picking out and organising the main ideas for an essay. In maths, he is criticised for the chaotic layout of his work but he finds it difficult to organise things in a way that is logical to other people. His family is very supportive and give him a lot of help with homework, so much so that teachers are sometimes misled into believing that he is coping well, until his difficulties are highlighted by his very poor performance in written exams.

Because he is so articulate, Michael is able to explain his frustrations to his teachers who are, on the whole, sympathetic. However, they are not very helpful in providing him with useful strategies.

Strategies

- The use of a laptop to record his work – especially one with a speech recognition software package.

- The use of creative and thinking skills strategies – especially synectics and classification exercises.

- Promote the use of collaborative group work.

- Explore with Michael memorisation techniques such as mind mapping, stories and visual associations.

- Work with the entire class on sorting and constructing paragraphs and essays.

- Provide Michael with diagrammatic summaries and study guides to allow him to engage in distance learning and support his revision.

Dyspraxia

The definition of dyspraxia used by the Dyspraxia Foundation is as follows:

An impairment or immaturity of the organisation of movement. It is an immaturity in the way the brain processes information, which results in messages not being properly or fully transmitted. Dyspraxia affects the planning of what to do. In many individuals there may be associated problems with language, perception and thought.

There may be as many as one in ten of the population affected by the condition. The condition is also sometimes referred to as developmental dyspraxia or developmental coordination disorder. Males are four times more likely to be affected than females. Statistically it is possible that there is one child, in every class of 30 children, with dyspraxia.

For the teacher of history key issues seem to be identifying and planning a piece of work, whether that is an essay or a source investigation, organising and sequencing information and thinking and memorisation skills.

Use the following ideas to help plan your lessons:

- Allow pupils extra time.

- Help pupils plan work – either collaboratively with other pupils or with the use of flow charts and stepped instructions.

- Use sequencing strategies with pupils and have a metacognitive debrief. What strategies can we use when we sequence information?

- Explore the use of memorisation strategies – mnemonics, mind mapping etc.

ADHD

ADHD can be a condition that is very disruptive to a pupil's education. It has three predominating characteristics:

- Inattention – Pupils find it difficult to concentrate on the task in hand, their mind wanders.

- Hyperactivity – These pupils are constantly on the go and they cannot sit still. Some disruption is low level, e.g. constant rocking on a chair, fiddling with materials etc. but it can be a lot worse, i.e. moving out of their place, running out of classrooms etc.

- Impulsivity – At times pupils seem to act before they think. They seem to have little idea of consequence to their actions. Sometimes they do not think of the consequences of their actions on others. They seem to have a limited grasp of deferred gratification. They will work for immediate success and not opt for work where, even if the rewards are great, they are longer to achieve.

Teaching strategies

- Work needs to be broken down into chunks as far as it can.

- Reward success and completion of short tasks.

- Allow for kinaesthetic activity – on a continuum of card sort to role-play.

Case study: Trevor, Year 8 (ADHD)

Trevor had the highest aggregated CATs score when he entered his comprehensive school but was described by his primary teachers as having a 'self-destruct button'. He is a bundle of contradictions. On good days he is capable of being charming and polite. Sometimes he becomes so engrossed in an activity that it is hard to draw him away from it. He loves books, especially those with detailed maps and diagrams in, and likes to share what he has found out with teachers and other adults. He is a natural actor and sings and looks like an angel.

Yet Trevor is equally capable of destroying a lesson with his extremely disruptive and increasingly dangerous behaviour. He will erupt from his chair and turn on a machine just as someone puts their hands near it. His science teachers have had to give up all practical lessons and lock the preparation room when he is around because he uses his intelligence and wide reading to destructive effect. He has an intense dislike of writing and rarely does class work or submits homework. In mental arithmetic he excels although he is reluctant to allow classmates many opportunities to show what they know.

For a small band of troublesome peers, he is a hero. Most other pupils laugh at his antics but find him very disturbing. They are rarely brave enough to offer criticism.

His mother will not acknowledge that there is a problem and refuses to consider medication or psychiatric help.

Strategies

- Investigate the possibility that he is dyslexic if this has not already been done.

- Agree a school-wide policy of support, and even containment.

- Prioritise what behaviour or work is to be achieved and put in place a reward system. It might be best to make no demands as far as written work is concerned until the behaviour has been dealt with.

- Invite his mother to sit in on some lessons where the problems are most severe and keep trying to work with her.

- Try to use visual sources – cartoons, maps and images to stimulate and engage him.

Learning mentors

Learning mentors are one of the three main strands of the Excellence in Cities (EiC) initiative. They work with teaching and pastoral staff to identify, assess and work with pupils who need help to overcome barriers to learning. These barriers can include, amongst others:

- behavioural problems

- bereavement

- difficulties at home

- problems transferring from primary to secondary school

- poor study or organisational skills.

Pupils suffering multiple disadvantages are a particular priority for support. The key focus of the work is supporting children and raising standards of achievement.

Learning mentors are making a significant effect on the attendance, behaviour, self-esteem and progress of the pupils they support . . . the most successful and highly valued strand of the EiC programme . . . In 95% of the survey schools, inspectors judged that the mentoring programme made a positive contribution to the mainstream provision of the school as a whole, and had a beneficial effect on the behaviour of individual pupils and on their ability to learn and make progress.

(Ofsted 2003: 46)

They free teachers to teach as well as transform young people's attitudes towards school, their ability to cope with the challenges that they face, and ultimately their ability to achieve their true potential.

Their work typically takes the form of regular one-to-one sessions with children identified as requiring help, during which the learning mentor and child will agree targets for areas of concern (e.g. attendance, behaviour and attainment), and talk through any concerns the child might have regarding learning.

Learning mentors will typically form a relationship with the child, school staff and parents or carers in order to improve the child's engagement with learning.

The able child might have additional pressures, as well as some or all of the ones mentioned above. These might include:

- workload issues and being unable to prioritise

- pressure from teachers all wanting that little bit extra – or expecting them to do well

- pressure for performance of grade rather than mastery of skills or development of interests

- social integration pressures – feeling unable to relate to others.

Case study from a learning mentor: Chloe, Year 10 (exceptionally gifted and talented)

Chloe excels in the classroom, on the sports field, on the stage, in music activities and socially. She is a natural leader, is often elected form captain, and is well liked by her peers and her teachers. When she is asked about the future and possible careers, she throws up her hands and laughs because she simply has too many options.

She has always produced high quality homework but recently standards have begun to slip. Her evenings and weekends are filled with activity – flute lessons, netball or tennis matches, Duke of Edinburgh Award Scheme and rehearsals for plays. Chloe is becoming interested in politics too and has begun to spend hours after school sitting on a wall hotly debating topical issues with some older boys. She has asked her parents if she can go to some political meetings.

Chloe's parents are quietly concerned. They know that their daughter has a voracious appetite for learning and activity of one sort or another, but they believe that the time has come for her to choose some and give up others. Her parents also believe that teachers need to be more sensitive to the pressures they place on Chloe. She is everyone's safe A* and teachers become alarmed when they see her backsliding.

Strategies

The learning mentor worked with Chloe on the following aspects:

- Try to resolve problems over clashing commitments, without pressuring Chloe.

- Work with Chloe and her parents to draw up a list of activities in which she will take a leading part and others that need to be put on hold for a while.

- Monitor her closely and alert others if she continues to take on too many activities or doesn't appear to be coping well.

- Teach her how to take shortcuts.

- Help her prioritise her work between that for which she will produce real excellence and that where she will produce the necessary requirements. A plan of her GCSE history syllabus and a skills matrix will help her prioritise her work.

- Help her understand that A* work has a criteria which is not necessarily characterised by her working at 100%.

Mentors are useful when meetings between gifted history students and their teachers do not take place as frequently as you would like. Often the students meet with the head of history only once or twice each year. This is not enough, as students want to discuss issues, ask for support, relay positive experiences and have a chance to feel valued. They will want to discuss the issues mentioned above. They might want to talk about career or university choices. A school could use a mix of staff mentors and the school's special educational needs coordinator (SENCO) for a mentoring project. The SENCO might provide packs for the mentors containing the following information:

- an IEP for each student

- SAT levels and raw scores

- CAT scores

- recent test/exam results

- copies of communications with parents since last review

- any other relevant documents.

In this way mentors will be supplied with information enabling them to build up a profile of each student, their strengths and any current weaknesses or areas for support.

A simple form could be provided to be completed by the mentor identifying current progress, student views/issues, targets and actions.

Case study – Using the SENCO and mentors

Eight teachers in a mentoring team were allocated a group of ten students across the age range. A gender balance was maintained as far as possible. Some effort was made to match a student's strengths with the mentors' specialisms. The mentors kept the same group of mentees each year, adding new Year 7 students as the Year 11 students moved on. A key aspect of the session was target setting, based on class activities.

A mentor typically saw two students per week during a 50 minute period. All staff in the team had 'mentoring time' on their timetable at the same time each week. The regular review sessions helped to identify and respond to individual needs of students who valued the opportunity to talk about their needs and support requests.

Although there was general confidentiality, some issues and their resolution might not have come to light without the mentoring opportunities. Before the project started there was no support for the G&T cohort, or discussion of progress, interests and needs. A two-way dialogue was established on a regular basis enabling far greater responsiveness to the needs of the cohort and greater awareness of the impact of the G&T programme.

Success factors included:

- the creation of a team of staff with the necessary qualities and experience

- safeguarded time which is always available for the mentoring project

- suitable places for the mentoring to take place which create a safe and confidential environment

- support from the senior management of the school.

School library

School libraries are a very underrated asset in a school. The problems with them tend to be:

- they are skewed to the upper end of the school. It is probably better if there is an independent sixth form library.

- they reflect the interests of the teachers and librarians rather than the children. Also these books can be academic.

- a dearth of suitable books. There seems to be a gap for books at Key Stages 3 and 4. Lots of them tend to repeat information in textbooks. Honourable exceptions are the Heinemann *History Eyewitness* series, but this is an underdeveloped area.

- limited ICT facilities. Even when the facilities are present there is a tendency for them to be underutilised – pupils are busy, but busy doing what?

To make library use more effective, it would be useful for the librarian to work with a group of able pupils looking into issues related to history. They might:

- be given budgetary control over a useful sum

- have a copy of the units covered at Key Stages 3 and 4 and post-16

- choose a range of resources that they think would be useful and appeal to pupils

- use ICT facilities in the library to investigate different websites and then to evaluate them for usefulness to the different topics being studied. This information could then be compiled as a favourites guide for others to use.

Links with parents

Parents are a child's primary educators. It is important to remember that the whole purpose of a school is to help a family to educate a child. With this in mind, we need to make use of all the talents that parents have, and encourage them to fully take part in the life of the school. This will only happen with active and open engagement with parents, focusing on the creation of excellence in all that children do.

Communication is a key factor. Parents need to know the expectations of the school and the school needs to know the expectations of the parents. Additionally parents need to know the ways in which they can legitimately help their children, especially the more able. If the school has aspirations to being a learning community then it might want to involve parents in learning as well.

History newsletters home might include:

- learning objectives and topics being covered that term/year

- details of any trips

- details of any deadlines for particular pieces of classwork or coursework

- information regarding learning styles – could a questionnaire be sent home, one that the parents could do themselves?

- lists of useful websites or other resources that cover a particular topic

- tips on how to help pupils revise for exams. How much time will children spend on it and how will you know if they have done it?

Diane Montgomery (2003) calls able pupils who have other special educational needs as being doubly exceptional. We must extend our repertoire to support them and other able pupils and other pupils in general. With the push on personalised learning and the workforce reforms it may be beyond the scope and time of individual teachers to do everything. However, what they will have to do is to lead and coordinate others to do this. The most precious attribute that teachers have is knowledge; knowledge of their pupils and pedagogical knowledge of how to help them. This knowledge will have to be taught to others. This places teachers, as ever, at the centre of this professional process, even if others tackle the day-to-day aspects. Teachers are crucial, essential and the lynchpin of our educational system. We should never forget that.

CHAPTER 6

Beyond the classroom

- Field visits
- Summer schools
- Masterclasses
- Links with universities
- School history clubs
- Homework

Chapter 4 presented a clear rationale for extending the level of challenge in the history classroom. In this chapter we consider how the learning of the able pupil can be developed outside the classroom through visits, summer schools and masterclasses. Nevertheless it should not be forgotten that many of the principles that were dealt with in Chapter 4, such as explicit learning and metacognition, puzzle, enquiry and construction of meaning, still hold true. This is a case of the classroom getting bigger rather than treating this as a separate entity. In any case it is the aim of this chapter to show how the learning of the able can be extended and enriched further.

Field visits

One of the strongest attractions that history has for many pupils is its practical feel. Field work and visits are an important part of many departments' work and they give valuable scope for the able pupil to extend their learning further.

The Schools History Project placed field work on the map. One component of its four unit course was entitled *History Around Us* and required pupils to study local history through a site visit.

History Around Us, published by Holmes McDougall in 1976, set four aims for the course:

1. To make pupils aware that the visible remains of the past around us are as important a resource for our understanding of history as written documents.

2. To give pupils the knowledge, skills and techniques so they can:

   a. identify the visible remains

   b. study and interpret them

   c. place them in their wider historical context.

3. To help pupils reconstruct the lives and purposes of people associated with historical sites at particular periods in the past.

4. To create an interest in and basis for further historical exploration of their environment which will continue beyond school.

Point 1 may seem a little naive in this age of *Time Team* but in general these points are a sound beginning. Point 2 is worth unpicking. A lot of time on field visits can be spent on identifying the remains. Pupils can go on field visits and spend a lot of time filling in worksheets that ask them to sketch and complete. Pupils might be directed to examine specific features of historical sites and say what they were or what they might have been used for.

Points 2b and 2c require more but they need unpicking. Study and interpret them can mean different things and it is certainly true that we would be using the term interpretation differently in 1976 to how we would use it today. Place them in a wider historical context might mean relating them to the period at the time, and perhaps complement this with further source material.

Point 3 has the whiff of empathy about it, but to consider how the physical remains of the past help us understand its social history and how it might show a society's *mentalité* is surely valid? Point 4 strikes a resonance with the current government's commitment to lifelong learning.

There was a divergence between sentiment and the reality. Page 95 provides an example of the kind of tasks that can be expected by pupils working at an abbey. After sketching out some introductory lessons, it was stipulated that the pupils could record information on their visit to the abbey viz.:

- The site of the abbey – Where is it and why was that particular location chosen? When was it built and by whom?

- The monastic buildings – Pupils could explore the abbey, finding and recording the different buildings and their features such as:

  - The church – Where were the altars, saints' shrines, night stairs, effigies and grave slabs, dividing screens? What is the plan of the church?

  - The cloister – Where are the chapter house, reredorters, sacristy, watering room, parlour, lavers, book cupboard?

- Outer buildings – Where are the kitchens, bakehouse, brewhouse, abbot's house, infirmary, guest house, barns, dovecote, fishpond, water mill, outer gate?

- Water supply and drainage – How did the abbey get its drinking water and water for ablutions? What architectural style are the buildings? What is the state of repair of the buildings?

- Other buildings – Is there a nearby hall or manor house which may have been built using stone and lead from the monastery?

These questions simply ask pupils to identify and map a worksheet as they go around the site. The follow-up work asked pupils to cross-reference their answers. In many senses the visit is redundant. The pupils could have got the required information from a well-informed guidebook. Our pupils, especially the more able, require more.

Chris Culpin, the current director of the Schools History Project, echoed and expanded these points. In *Teaching History 97* (November 1999) he wrote an article entitled 'No puzzle, no learning: how to make your site visits rigorous, fascinating and indispensable'. In this article he argued that for a site visit to be successful it should:

1. be presented as a puzzle

2. develop site investigation skills, including cross-referencing with written and other types of documentary evidence

3. depend upon and exploit prior learning

4. find out about people in the past and their world views

5. provide the basis for exploring other themes and dimensions of history, for example citizenship and the relevance of the past with the present.

The first point is absolutely crucial. An essential way of establishing challenge for our able learners is by creating cognitive conflict and mental anguish. This is needed if they are to do more than simply process and replicate information. It is a vital ingredient if they are to create meaning and understanding (see Chapter 4 for a fuller discussion of this). Culpin gives some examples:

- Chedworth, in Gloucestershire, has been presented as a Roman villa, but if this is the case then why are there two dining rooms, lots of small rooms, but no larger suites of rooms?

- Tintagel – a Celtic monastery or were the 'monks' cells' accommodation for thirteenth century castle-builders? How might we test these conflicting ideas?

- Cotehele – is it a late medieval manor house or an eighteenth century reconstruction medieval manor house?

The result of these kinds of enquiry is that it forces pupils to examine a site for a purpose. Information is collated and collected with a view of supporting or contradicting a particular idea. It encourages pupils to pose their own questions in the light of a line of enquiry and depending upon the answers they find themselves getting. Such an approach will require students to blend the use of documentary evidence to support or contradict ideas, answer questions and suggest new lines of enquiry. Pupils should find themselves going back and forth between site and documents to reach a final, plausible if not definitive conclusion.

Point 3 expands the point that pupils need to prepare for a site visit. This can be thought of in at least two ways. First of all there is the acquisition of contextual knowledge. To investigate a monastery pupils might need to know:

- who the monks were, what they believed and their daily routine

- technical terms such as cloister, transept, presbytery, Cluniac, etc.

- some of the ideas that the Church had at the time – perception of a world view of charity, heaven, hell, intercessionary saints and purgatory for example

- some of the building techniques and architectural practices that were common in the period.

The second way is to generate a set of hypotheses about the site and the puzzle it might present. Pupils should be encouraged to examine complementary source material before the visit. This can help them define the lines of enquiry that they want to pursue. It might help them support or contradict these hypotheses and present a focus.

There is a clear pitfall with hypotheses testing. It is not uncommon to set two diametrically opposed hypotheses for the pupils to test. The mark scheme then rewards those candidates that recognise the deficiencies in those hypotheses and construct their own. The potential pitfall with this approach is that the initial hypotheses are so different from each other that pupils will trigger a third hypothesis without really having to think about it. A caricature might be:

The monks were very rich and lived lives of luxury. They were only concerned with themselves.

The monks were pious people who spent the day praying and doing charitable acts.

From these two statements the pupils are asked to construct a third; a compromise between two extreme positions. The reason that this kind of thing does not work is that it is ahistorical. The resulting hypothesis that pupils construct is likely to be ahistorical as well. What we want to do is get the pupils to use their historical knowledge and understanding as a way of explaining a tension or puzzle.

For example, an investigation of Castle Acre priory might want pupils to investigate the tension of how could Cluniac monks, who were supposed to lead an austere life, live in a place of such great wealth?

Pupils might be asked to investigate:

- How did the priory support a life of holiness?

- How can we tell how the monks lived?

- What seemed to be important to the monks?

- How did the monastery project an image of power?

- What are the symbols within the priory?

- What do we think the monks believed?

- How can we tell the prior was an important man?

- Why do we think that by the sixteenth century the priory was being criticised?

This could be developed into a continuity and change theme by comparing the prior's house to the original eleventh century buildings – e.g. the church.

After examining the hypothesis, or being required to explain the tension, pupils could draw up a set of tentative answers and explore them together back in the classroom. Guidebooks and volumes such as G. R. Evans, *Faith in the Medieval World* (2002), and Richard Taylor, *How to Read a Church* (2003), can all provide clues of how to approach the site as a manifestation of a particular world view that needs unlocking to the pupils.

Summer schools

History summer schools are not a very common phenomenon. Money tends to go towards summer schools which support pupil progress in literacy, numeracy and science. The following case studies originate from Hertfordshire LA in the year 2002. They show us what might be possible. All these summer schools model a close theme of collaboration – 60 schools in the case of Duxford, or a cross-phase or cross-subject theme. They all allowed pupils to socialise and produce outcomes to a higher level than they would in the classroom. With the development, at last, of humanities specialist schools it is hoped and anticipated this will become more common with the support of the Specialist Schools Trust.

The following examples are taken from Hertfordshire LA website and show what can be achieved by schools, LAs and their able pupils in history.

Duxford airshow

Sixty pupils from a dozen schools came together at Duxford to explore propaganda and artefacts from twentieth century warfare. Pupils had the opportunity to hear recordings from the period, look at clips of film and handle newspapers from the Second World War period. They were also able to handle and investigate military equipment and weapons used by allied forces.

After lunch the afternoon began with a warm-up Morse code challenge in which each team was given a signal to transmit and receive across a runway.

During the afternoon pupils explored the aircraft collections at Duxford investigating the uses of various aircraft and drawing conclusions about their manufacture and use. To end the day pupils were asked to assess what they had seen and plan a display using just five of the items on display at Duxford which they thought would most appropriately encapsulate and effectively communicate the most significant aspects of warfare in the twentieth century.

'Communications and war'

This summer school was designed for 35 students from Years 6 and 7 and centred around an early visit to Bletchley Park. The students were asked to work in teams for the duration of the summer school, giving a competitive feel to the tasks. Students had the opportunity to learn about, and experiment with, various forms of communication ranging from semaphore to ICT. Sessions included language awareness, debating skills and practice, electronics and circuit boards, problem solving, code breaking, T-shirt printing and a historical background to the Bletchley Park visit. Other opportunities were presented by the use of drama based upon the war theme including character analysis, costume, scriptwriting and interpreting sources.

The place of the Church in medieval Europe and 'surviving France'

Week 1 of the summer school explored medieval European life with a particular focus upon the importance of the Church and its work. Week 2 continued the European theme by focusing on aspects of conversational French so that students could visit a medieval cathedral in Normandy.

Masterclasses

Traditionally the core subjects have benefited from masterclass activities. An outside expert has come into the school and worked on a particular aspect of learning with able pupils. However there is no reason why the same cannot happen with history as a subject area. The golden rules for this kind of work seem to be:

1. Pupils need to have a demonstrable benefit from this. They need to be able to produce an outcome that they would not otherwise be able to do in ordinary class time.

2. There should be a focus on collaboration and social interaction. One benefit to pupils might be working with other pupils, who at this time have been identified as able.

3. There should be an opportunity to increase the level of challenge.

4. There should be an opportunity to encourage the breadth and depth of learning.

5. There should be the opportunity to encourage a degree of reflection about what it means to study history.

6. There may be the opportunity to develop a cross-curricular link.

Case study 1: Art and cultural history

In school A teachers had been asked to nominate pupils for a curriculum extension group. Three groups were established – one for each year group in Key Stage 3. Two teachers were assigned to each group. The Year 8 teachers decided that they would focus on the *Making and Meaning Exhibition* that was currently at the National Gallery in London. Pupils studied works as diverse as *The Wilton Diptych* and Turner's *The Fighting Temeraire*. Pupils researched and found out about the circumstances in which the painting was made. They investigated the symbolism of the painting and sought meaning in it. They placed the painting into a wider context of history and the history of art. The course lasted four days and included a trip to the National Gallery in London to review the work.

1. The outcome was different to what they were able to produce in ordinary class time. Pupils produced sensitive pieces of work reflecting how they felt about a piece of art. They were able to analyse visual constructions and seek understanding from the abstract. They were able to treat these sources as representations of cultural history. This is an area of study which can be neglected in the busy history department.

2. There was social work and collaboration. They were able to work together in groups and visit an external site. They were able to present their findings in a way which was personal to them.

3. This was a challenging piece of work. Pupils were required to work at the higher ends of Bloom's taxonomy. They were asked to seek patterns and meanings – **analysis**. They were required to justify why they had interpreted the painting in certain ways – **evaluation**.

4. Breadth and depth of learning were achieved in this project because pupils studied an aspect of the past through a medium which may not be that common. Secondly depth was achieved because they looked at one source and criss-crossed it by placing it in a firm historical context.

Case study 2: Comparative history

In school B a group of Year 8 pupils were taken off timetable in their history lessons. These pupils were asked to test a model for explaining colonisations. They went through the model so that they understood it. They were then asked to apply the model in different historical settings: the Roman conquest of Britain; the Norman conquest of England; the Spanish conquest of South America and the British conquest of India. The information they were given on each case study was carefully structured and limited so as not to swamp the pupils. They were asked to apply the model in each instance and reflect upon how effective it was. They were asked to seek analogy and anomalies, to determine whether the weaknesses of the models outstripped its strengths. This had a direct impact on their thinking. They had to consider whether an exception to the rule meant that the rule was useless. They had to decide whether they could have a best fit explanatory model. This led some of them to consider the differences between explanations in history and science. They examined how the uniqueness of a historical event detracted from an overall generalisation. They were forced to think in terms of balance and exceptions rather than absolutes.

1. The outcome was different to what they were able to produce under normal classroom conditions. The work was analytical and involved examining relationships and comparing and contrasting. Pupils looked for subtle differences and nuances of meaning.

2. Pupils were working with other able pupils in small groups.

3. There was challenge and rigour with the task. As has already been intimated pupils were asked to change the normal mode of their thinking.

4. Breadth and depth were achieved because pupils had to study a range of different case studies in depth, some of which they might not have examined before, and make direct comparisons which encourages breadth.

5. There was an encouragement to think about what it might mean to study history because pupils were required to think about how we explain events in history. They were required to think about how far we can make generalisations in history and how far we deal with unique discrete events.

6. The construction of analytical tools and models is arguably a tool taken from the social sciences.

Case study 3: Heritage and history

In the March 2005 edition of *Teaching History – Re-thinking Differentiation*, Neal Watkin and Johannes Ahrenfelt wrote an article entitled 'Mixing a G and T cocktail: teaching about heritage through a cross-curricular enquiry'. In this article they discussed a unit of work which an able Year 8 group participated in. They had to determine a vision for their home town of Dereham in Norfolk. This vision of the future was based upon an appreciation of past societies – what type of Dereham would they like to see for the future – and what aspects of Dereham's heritage would they like to preserve or develop. An important aspect of the project was the way that pupils were asked to set their own targets (next steps for learning). After a significant introduction pupils studied various historical forms of society. This included Marx's idea of *Communism*, J. J. Rousseau's *Social Contract*, Machiavelli's *The Prince* and the concept of Fascism. They then tried to define what they thought a perfect society might look like. The next stage was to use a range of source material to investigate aspects of Dereham's past to determine what its significant events were. They then invited the clerk of Dereham Council to a lesson where he answered questions on how the district council planned for the future and dealt with issues to do with heritage and preservation. The class were then put into groups and had control of form of the outcome: a presentation of their vision of Dereham in 2020.

1. The outcome was different to what they were able to produce in ordinary class time. Pupils produced sensitive pieces of work reflecting how they felt about the future, how society should work and what needs to be preserved of the past.

2. There was social work and collaboration. They were able to work together in groups and visit an external site. They were able to present their findings in a way which was personal to them.

3. This was a challenging piece of work. Pupils were required to work at the higher ends of Bloom's taxonomy. They were asked to seek patterns and meanings – **analysis**. They were required to justify why they had interpreted the painting in certain ways – **evaluation**. They were asked to predict and engage in 'blue sky' thinking. Perhaps, most importantly, they were asked to place a personal value on the past.

4. Breadth and depth of learning were achieved in this project because pupils studied an aspect of the past through a medium which may not be that common. Secondly depth was achieved because they looked at one source and criss-crossed it by placing it in a firm historical context.

It is the firm belief of the author that what counts the most for the able child is the experience they get in their ordinary classrooms. However, what the three case studies above illustrate is the value of enriching the experiences that our able and gifted pupils get. All these case studies show the benefit of collaborative learning, cross–curricular or thematic learning and how to make pupils think harder and deeper. This was all achieved without reference to a grade or pupil 'performance' but by mastery and a love of learning.

Links with universities

The local university can be an extremely useful resource for the department. It might be possible to establish a link with the local university/HE institution so that:

- Experts could visit the school and classes. There is a temptation to use these people only with the sixth form but it might be possible to use undergraduates with lower school classes.

- Some lecturers/graduate students/undergraduates might be working in the field of heritage studies. They might actually be doing work/investigations on museums, galleries and field sites in your area. Would it be possible for these people to work with your able pupils in small groups to assist them with site investigations, dealing with historical significance and interpretation?

- Are there undergraduates who are seeking a career in teaching? Is it possible to use them as assistants in small group work in some way?

- Is it possible for older students to use the university library as a resource for individual assignments?

- Is it possible to link the school and university history clubs? Could the university host the school in some way?

- Can the university students help provide a set of role models as to the accessibility and value of higher education to those able pupils who do not come from a social group that normally enters it?

School history clubs

An effective school history club is worth its weight in gold in many different ways. It provides an excellent basis for pupils to develop their interests further. It provides an excellent opportunity for able pupils to interact with each other and for older pupils to take on a leadership role. The following principles can make the difference between success and disaster.

1. Pupils should take ownership and run the club. This is an ideal opportunity for older pupils to develop and exercise leadership skills. A formal committee should be established with designated roles: chairperson, secretary, treasurer, resources officer, events organiser etc.

2. The committee should organise a programme of meetings. These are normally to take place in school time. However, it is possible that there might be events after school and/or during the weekends, although this is dependent upon staff support. Ideally these events should follow a theme. This might not be the same as a period or topic, but there should be some element of coherence.

3. School meetings should provide a mixture of opportunity. There should be a fun element – perhaps to watch and debate an historical film, play games or an opportunity to have a coursework or homework clinic.

4. The idea of mentoring and support is crucial. What can elevate a club from somewhere children have fun and relax socially (although that is an

important and worthy aim in itself) is for some, if not all, children to develop an historical area of interest. This area of interest might be initiated by a wider access to historical knowledge. Talking to a sixth former or GCSE student can whet the appetite of younger pupils (to realise that they have only scratched the surface of their studies and that there is a huge wealth of learning that they can access later). It also might be that older pupils can mentor more able younger pupils in developing their areas of interest. Can a member of the lower sixth planning her own individual study on the Crusades help an able Year 7 pupil 'find out more' about the course of the First Crusade or medieval heresy? A further possibility is that the well-taught and independent learner in the sixth form will model appropriate learning skills, procedures and questions unconsciously. This means that this is another opportunity for pupils to access, replicate and learn necessary skills.

5. Collaboration – An alternative approach to lots of discrete and individual study is for the whole club to engage in a collaborative theme. It is tempting to make this a local history project but it need not necessarily be so. Good examples of local history projects might include: producing a tourist guide book for the local area (could funding be attracted to publish this?); an oral history project to investigate how life has changed in the local area; an investigation of a local notable or local historical site. On a wider scale there may be an opportunity to study a local aspect of a national theme, such as the impact of two world wars on the local community, or a study of the Great Plague of 1665 through London. This could be done by evaluating Daniel Defoe's *Journal of the Plague Year* and a walk through and to the major Wren churches in London.

6. Involvement with local bodies and experts. The local historical society can be a very useful link. They may be able to provide you with guest speakers, to be used with caution. More importantly they may be able to put you in touch with contacts and resources that will allow you to develop areas of interest further. The local branch of the Historical Association will be able to function in much the same way.

7. Competitions. A key theme of this book has been that able pupils should re-orientate themselves away from performance criteria towards mastery of specific knowledge, skills and concepts. However, performance can still, in some circumstances, be seen as an important motivator. The journal *Teaching History* regularly advertises competitions such as ones run by the Spirit of Normandy Trust. These are normally essay competitions but the research, planning and discussion work beforehand can be a good theme for a history club.

Homework

Homework can be of educational benefit to many pupils. Amongst the chief benefits of setting pupils homework seem to be:

- it can consolidate learning in the classroom

- it can extend and deepen learning in the classroom

- it can ask pupils to apply their learning to a different context

- pupils can develop and increase their capacity to work independently or carry out research work

- preparing pupils for expectations of GCSE, AS/A2 and university courses.

Generalisations from school homework policies suggest that it should:

- last for a set amount of time

- be done at home

- be unmediated – done by the pupils themselves

- be set regardless of how appropriate it fits into the context of the lesson

- be monitored for completion, marked and graded.

The potential pitfall is that some homework set does not comply with the first set of bullet points. The single biggest inhibitor is that it is unmediated. There is no teacher present to guide the pupil. Secondly pupils themselves generally have low levels of independent learning skills. This means that the menu of homework activity a teacher can choose from becomes limited. This narrows further when one places the constraints of the second set of bullet points. A twenty-minute unmediated task suggests an even more limited set of tasks that can be done. Application and independent tasks are more challenging and it is at this point that pupils are more likely to want to ask specific help from a teacher or other adult.

This is compounded with the notion that not all pupils have access to the facilities that allow for independent academic work. Quiet time and space can be a luxury in many households.

However, if we are to recognise that homework can provide an opportunity for pupil learning then these points ought to be considered:

- Integration with classroom activity. I do not think that homework should be an additional task set from the context of a single lesson, but a continuing project that can be done over a term. If this is the case then how it dovetails with the course as a whole, how it is set up, the modelling of quality, tutorial time, assessment of first drafts are all crucial. This has to be a meaningful piece of work.

- Liaison with parents. A letter home outlining the project being done, resources needed, deadline dates for pieces of the project and the expectation of how many hours over the term the piece of work might take are all important.

- Liaison with other school bodies such as the ICT department and school library regarding the availability of resources.

- The use of place in school to allow pupils to work during and immediately after school hours.

- The use of a school history club to provide peer mentoring support and additional resources.

The scope for increasing the learning experience of able pupils outside the classroom is large. But it should be remembered that this has to be a meaningful experience that takes and extends the learning further. More importantly this area tends to be the focus of many schools' gifted and talented policy, but it is only a fraction of the time that a pupil will spend in school. What is more significant are the ways of increasing the level of challenge in everyday lessons as outlined in Chapter 4.

Appendices

Institutional quality standards in gifted and talented education

Generic Elements	Entry	Developing	Exemplary
	A – Effective teaching and learning strategies		
1. Identification	i. The school/college has learning conditions and systems to identify gifted and talented pupils in all year groups and an agreed definition and shared understanding of the meaning of 'gifted and talented' within its own, local and national contexts.	i. Individual pupils are screened annually against clear criteria at school/college and subject/topic level.	i. **Multiple criteria and sources of evidence** are used to identify gifts and talents, including through the use of a broad range of quantitative and qualitative data.
	ii. An **accurate record** of the identified gifted and talented population is kept and updated.	ii. The record is used to identify under-achievement and **exceptional achievement** (both within and outside the population) and to track/review pupil **progress.**	ii. The record is supported by a comprehensive monitoring, progress planning and reporting system which all staff regularly share and contribute to.
	iii. The identified gifted and talented population broadly reflects the school/college's **social and economic composition**, gender and ethnicity.	iii. **Identification** systems address issues of **multiple exceptionality** (pupils with specific gifts/talents and special educational needs).	iii. Identification processes are regularly reviewed and refreshed in the light of pupil performance and value-added data. The gifted and talented population is fully repre-sentative of the school/college's population.
Evidence			
Next steps			
2. Effective provision in the classroom	i. The school/college addresses the different needs of the gifted and talented population by providing a stimulating learning environment and by extending the teaching repertoire.	i. Teaching and learning strategies are diverse and flexible, meeting the needs of distinct pupil groups within the gifted and talented population (e.g. able underachievers, exceptionally able).	i. The school/college has established a range of methods to find out what works best in the classroom, and shares this within the school/college and with other schools and colleges.
	ii. Teaching and learning is differentiated and delivered through both individual and group activities.	ii. A range of challenging learning and teaching strategies is evident in lesson planning and delivery. **Independent learning** skills are developed.	ii. Teaching and learning are suitably challenging and varied, incorporating the breadth, depth and pace required to progress high achievement. Pupils routinely work independently and self-reliantly.

	Entry	Developing	Exemplary
	iii. Opportunities exist to extend learning through **new technologies**.	iii. The use of **new technologies** across the curriculum is focused on **personalised learning** needs.	iii. The innovative use of new technologies raises the achievement and motivation of gifted and talented pupils.
Evidence			
Next steps			
3. Standards	i. Levels of **attainment** and **achievement** for gifted and talented pupils are comparatively high in relation to the rest of the school/college population and are in line with those of similar pupils in similar schools/colleges.	i. Levels of **attainment** and **achievement** for gifted and talented pupils are broadly consistent across the gifted and talented population and above those of similar pupils in similar schools/colleges.	i. Levels of attainment and achievement for gifted and talented pupils indicate sustainability over time and are well above those of similar pupils in similar schools/colleges.
	ii. Self-evaluation indicates that gifted and talented provision is satisfactory.	ii. Self-evaluation indicates that gifted and talented provision is good.	ii. Self-evaluation indicates that gifted and talented provision is very good or excellent.
	iii. Schools/colleges' gifted and talented education programmes are explicitly linked to the achievement of SMART outcomes and these highlight improvements in pupils' attainment and achievement.		
Evidence			
Next steps			
B – Enabling curriculum entitlement and choice			
4. Enabling curriculum entitlement and choice	i. Curriculum organisation is flexible, with opportunities for enrichment and increasing subject/topic choice. Pupils are provided with support and guidance in making choices.	i. The curriculum offers opportunities and guidance to pupils which enable them to work beyond their age and/or phase, and across subjects or topics, according to their aptitudes and interests.	i. The curriculum offers personalised learning pathways for pupils which maximise individual potential, retain flexibility of future choices, extend well beyond test/examination requirements and result in sustained impact on pupil attainment and achievement.
Evidence			
Next steps			

Definitions for words and phrases in bold are provided in the glossary in the Quality Standards *User Guide*, available at www2.teachernet.gov.uk/gat. QS Model October 2005

Generic Elements	Entry	Developing	Exemplary
		C – Assessment for learning	
5. Assessment for learning	i. Processes of data analysis and pupil assessment are employed throughout the school/college to plan learning for gifted and talented pupils.	i. Routine progress reviews, using both qualitative and quantitative data, make effective use of prior, predictive and value-added attainment data to plan for progression in pupils' learning.	i. Assessment data are used by teachers and across the school/college to ensure challenge and sustained progression in individual pupils' learning.
	ii. Dialogue with pupils provides focused feedback which is used to plan future learning.	ii. Systematic oral and written feedback helps pupils to set challenging curricular targets.	ii. Formative assessment and individual target-setting combine to maximise and celebrate pupils' achievements.
	iii. Self and peer assessment, based on clear understanding of criteria, are used to increase pupils' responsibility for learning.	iii. Pupils reflect on their own skill development and are involved in the design of their own targets and tasks.	iii. Classroom practice regularly requires pupils to reflect on their own progress against targets, and engage in the direction of their own learning.
Evidence			
Next steps			
6. Transfer and transition	i. Shared processes, using agreed criteria, are in place to ensure the productive transfer of information from one setting to another (i.e. from class to class, year to year and school/college to school/college).	i. Transfer information concerning gifted and talented pupils, including parental input, informs targets for pupils to ensure progress in learning. Particular attention is given to including new admissions.	i. Transfer data concerning gifted and talented pupils are used to inform planning of teaching and learning at subject/aspect/topic and individual pupil level, and to ensure progression according to ability rather than age or phase.
Evidence			
Next steps			
		D – School/College organisation	
7. Leadership	i. A named member of the governing body, senior management team and the lead professional responsible for gifted and talented education have clearly directed responsibilities for motivating and driving gifted and talented provision. The head teacher actively champions gifted and talented provision.	i. Responsibility for gifted and talented provision is distributed, and evaluation of its impact shared, at all levels in the school/college. Staff subscribe to policy at all levels. Governors play a significant supportive and evaluative role.	i. Organisational structures, communication channels and the deployment of staff (e.g. workforce remodelling) are flexible and creative in supporting the delivery of personalised learning. Governors take a lead in celebrating achievements of gifted and talented pupils.
Evidence			
Next steps			

	Entry	Developing	Exemplary
8. Policy	i. The gifted and talented policy is integral to the school/college's inclusion agenda and approach to personalised learning, feeds into and from the single school/college improvement plan and is consistent with other policies.	i. The policy directs and reflects best practice in the school/college, is regularly reviewed and is clearly linked to other policy documentation.	i. The policy includes input from the whole school/college community and is regularly refreshed in the light of innovative national and international practice.
Evidence			
Next steps			
9. School/college ethos and pastoral care	i. The school/college sets high expectations, recognises achievement and celebrates the successes of all its pupils. ii. The school/college identifies and addresses the particular social and emotional needs of gifted and talented pupils in consultation with pupils, parents and carers.	i. The school/college fosters an environment which promotes positive behaviour for learning. Pupils are listened to and their views taken into account. ii. Strategies exist to counteract bullying and any adverse effects of social and curriculum pressures. Specific support for able underachievers and pupils from different cultures and social backgrounds is available and accessible.	i. An ethos of ambition and achievement is agreed and shared by the whole school/college community. Success across a wide range of abilities is celebrated. ii. The school/college places equal emphasis on high achievement and emotional well-being, underpinned by programmes of support personalised to the needs of gifted and talented pupils. There are opportunities for pupils to use their gifts to benefit other pupils and the wider community.
Evidence			
Next steps			
10. Staff development	i. Staff have received professional development in meeting the needs of gifted and talented pupils.	i. The induction programme for new staff addresses gifted and talented issues, both at whole school/college and specific subject/aspect level.	i. There is ongoing audit of staff needs and an appropriate range of professional development in gifted and talented education. Professional development is informed by research and collaboration within and beyond the school/college.

Definitions for words and phrases in bold are provided in the glossary in the Quality Standards *User Guide*, available at www2.teachernet.gov.uk/gat. QS Model October 2005

Generic Elements	Entry	Developing	Exemplary
	ii. The lead professional responsible for gifted and talented education has received appropriate professional development.	ii. Subject/aspect and phase leaders have received specific professional development in meeting the needs of gifted and talented pupils.	ii. Priorities for the development of gifted and talented provision are included within a professional development entitlement for all staff and are monitored through performance management processes.
Evidence			
Next steps			
11. Resources	i. Provision for gifted and talented pupils is supported by appropriate budgets and resources.	i. Allocated resources include school/college based and nationally available resources, and these have a significant and measurable impact on the progress that pupils make and their attitudes to learning.	i. Resources are used to stimulate innovative and experimental practice, which is shared throughout the school/college and which are regularly reviewed for impact and best value.
Evidence			
Next steps			
12. Monitoring and evaluation	i. Subject and phase audits focus on the quality of teaching and learning for gifted and talented pupils. Whole-school/college targets are set using prior attainment data. ii. Elements of provision are planned against clear objectives within effective whole-school self-evaluation processes.	i. Performance against targets (including at pupil level) is regularly reviewed. Targets include qualitative pastoral and curriculum outcomes as well as numerical data. ii. All elements, including non-academic aspects of gifted and talented provision, are planned to clear objectives and are subjected to detailed evaluation.	i. Performance against targets is rigorously evaluated against clear criteria. Qualitative and quantitative outcomes inform whole-school/college self-evaluation processes. ii. The school/college examines and challenges its own provision to inform development of further experimental and innovative practice in collaboration with other schools/colleges.
Evidence			
Next steps			

E – Strong partnerships beyond the school

13. Engaging with the community, families and beyond	i. Parents/carers are aware of the school's/college's policy on gifted and talented provision, contribute to its identification processes and are kept informed of developments in gifted and talented provision, including through the School Profile.	i. Progression of gifted and talented pupils is enhanced by home-school/college partnerships. There are strategies to engage and support hard-to-reach parents/carers.	i. Parents/carers are actively engaged in extending provision. Support for gifted and talented provision is integrated with other children's services (e.g. Sure Start, EAL, traveller, refugee, LAC Services).
	ii. The school/college shares good practice and has some collaborative provision with other schools, colleges and the wider community.	ii. A coherent strategy for networking with other schools, colleges and local community organisations extends and enriches provision.	ii. There is strong emphasis on collaborative and innovative working with other schools/colleges which impacts on quality of provision locally, regionally and nationally.
Evidence			
Next steps			
14. Learning beyond the classroom	i. There are opportunities for pupils to learn beyond the school/college day and site (extended hours and out-of-school activities).	i. A coherent programme of enrichment and extension activities (through extended hours and out-of-school activities) complements teaching and learning and helps identify pupils' latent gifts and talents.	i. Innovative models of learning beyond the classroom are developed in collaboration with local and national schools/colleges to further enhance teaching and learning.
	ii. Pupils participate in dedicated gifted and talented activities (e.g. summer schools) and their participation is recorded.	ii. Local and national provision helps meet individual pupil's learning needs e.g. NAGTY membership, accessing outreach, local enrichment programmes.	ii. Coherent strategies are used to direct and develop individual expert performance via external agencies e.g. HE/FE links, on line support, and local/regional/national programmes.
Evidence			
Next steps			

Definitions for words and phrases in bold are provided in the glossary in the Quality Standards *User Guide*, available at www2.teachernet.gov.uk/gat. QS Model October 2005
© Crown copyright 2005–2007

Coaching

What is it?

Coaching is a loose term. It is sometimes seen as being synonymous with mentoring, counselling or classroom-based training. Definitions vary but there do seem to be some underlying characteristics and principles which make a coaching programme effective. Coaching is:

● classroom based

● pedagogically focused

● non-judgemental

● analytical in nature

● about allowing the teacher who is being coached to reflect upon their practice

● about enabling teachers to translate reflections and theory into classroom practice

● about creating sustainable development rather than surface change.

Why do it?

We have found in our own school improvement work that it is the facilitation of peer coaching that enables teachers to extend their repertoire of teaching skills and **to transfer them from different classroom settings to others.**

From our experience, coaching contributes to transfer of training in five ways. In particular, teachers who are coached:

● generally practise new strategies more frequently and develop greater skill

● use their newly learned strategies more appropriately than 'uncoached' teachers

● exhibit greater long-term knowledge retention and skill regarding those strategies in which they have been coached

● are much more likely than 'uncoached' teachers to teach new models of learning to their students

● exhibit clearer understandings with regarding the purposes and uses of the new strategies.

During the implementation of this approach during our Improving the Quality of Education for All school improvement projects we have made refinements in the use of peer coaching to support student learning. We have found that when the refinements noted below are incorporated into a school improvement design, **peer coaching can virtually assure 'transfer of training' for everyone.** In particular:

● peer coaching teams of two or three are much more effective than larger groups

● these groups are more effective when the entire staff are engaged in school improvement

● peer coaching works better when the senior management team participate in training and practice

- the effects are greater when formative study of student learning is embedded in the process.

Although peer coaching is an essential component of staff development, it also needs to be connected to other elements in order to form an effective school improvement strategy.

(Source: David Hopkins, Alma Harris *et al.* (2000) *Creating the Conditions for Teaching and Learning*. David Fulton Publishers.)

In short even though it is expensive in terms of time and staff commitment it provides 'good value for money' because of the impact that it has. It is virtually the only effective form of CPD that develops teacher knowledge, skills and expertise to the point where they are no longer replicating isolated strategies but instead they are able to draw upon an extended explicit repertoire of learning models and are able to blend them for best use with their children.

How do we do it?

The model that the author favours is a peer coaching programme. Staff are paired, or alternatively they work in threes. Each person coaches and is coached. The process involves:

- a joint planning session. This allows the coach to influence the planning process and by questioning it helps the coached teacher make explicit the thinking and assumptions that they have regarding their lesson planning.
- the lesson is observed and perhaps videotaped.
- post-lesson discussion. At this point the coach helps the coached teacher unpick their lesson to look at the impact of their teaching on the pupils' learning. Together they consider the possible consequences of alternative teaching strategies and interventions.

What impact is it going to have?

Long term:

- raised pupil outcomes
- long term sustainable change by teachers
- increasing the internal capacity of a school to implement change
- effective practice to be shared, disseminated and constructed through the school
- creating a common language about pedagogy in the school
- increasing the self-efficacy of individual teachers
- developing corporate efficacy.

Short term:

- increased repertoire of skills demonstrated by teachers
- targeting of 'pinch points' in teaching and learning
- an increase of enthusiasm.

Auditing provision for the most able students in history at Key Stages 3–4

Stage 1

The more able cohort in your department/subject

If you have identified your top 5–10% (your more able or gifted and talented cohort) in each year group, look critically at the composition of that cohort to see if any groups of pupils are under-represented in your subject.

	Y7	Y8	Y9	Y10	Y11
% of pupils in each year group who receive free school meals					
% of pupils in the more able cohort who receive free school meals					
% of boys in each year group					
% of boys in the more able cohort in each year group					
% of girls in each year group					
% of girls in the more able cohort in each year group					
% of ethnic minority pupils in each year group					
% of ethnic minority pupils in the more able cohort in each year group					

Current levels of attainment

Percentages of pupils attaining Level 6 or above at the end of Key Stage 3

Attainment in KS3 teacher assessments:	National averages		
	Above	**In line**	**Below**
% of all pupils achieving Level 6 and above was:			
% of boys achieving Level 6 and above was:			
% of girls achieving Level 6 and above was:			

Take-up of subject at GCSE and post-16

Subject	% of pupils taking subject at KS4	% boys taking subject at KS4	% of girls taking subject at KS4

 From *Meeting the Needs of Your Most Able Pupils: History*, Routledge 2007

Subject	% of pupils taking subject post-16	% of boys taking subject post-16	% of girls taking subject post-16

Attitude to learning

In general, how do the most able pupils react to the subject?

(a) Enthusiastic	(b) Non-committal	(c) Disengaged

If (b) or (c), can you pinpoint why?

....

....

....

Extracurricular

What extracurricular support/activities are provided for the most able in each year group? (Include clubs, masterclasses, extension classes, visits, invited experts, links with business/colleges etc.)

Year	Extracurricular support/activity
Year 7	
Year 8	
Year 9	
Year 10	
Year 11	

From *Meeting the Needs of Your Most Able Pupils: History*, Routledge 2007

General

	Questions to ask	Yes/No/In progress	Priority for action
1.	Has the department developed a policy on its provision for the more able?		
2.	Does it have a more able/G&T coordinator or representative who liaises directly with the school more able/G&T coordinator?		
3.	Are the most able students clearly identified in subject registers?		
4.	Has the department identified CPD requirements in relation to more able pupils?		
5.	Has the department agreed the strategies it will use to provide suitable pace, depth and breadth for the most able?		
6.	Does the department have an agreed approach to providing for the exceptional child whose needs might not easily be met in the ordinary classroom?		
7.	Does short-term planning outline expectations for the most able and any extended/modified tasks for them?		
8.	Are there suitable resources for the most able?		
9.	Is homework used to extend the most able?		
10.	Do the most able have plenty of opportunities to develop as independent learners?		
11.	Are different learning styles taken into account when planning for and assessing the most able?		
12.	Do you keep a portfolio of outstanding work in your department?		
13.	Is provision for the most able regularly discussed at departmental meetings?		
14.	Do you share good practice in more able provision with other departments or schools?		
15.	Is the progress of your most able students effectively monitored?		

 From *Meeting the Needs of Your Most Able Pupils: History*, Routledge 2007

Stage 2

Highlight all areas where achievement or provision in your department is lacking. Decide on about three priorities to raise standards or improve provision for your most able and draw up an action plan making it clear:

- what your success criteria are or what you hope to achieve

- what action will be taken

- when the action will be taken and by whom

- where you will go for help

- what resources you need

- how you will monitor your progress

- what your deadline is for assessing your success.

From *Meeting the Needs of Your Most Able Pupils: History*, Routledge 2007

Creating progress

The following extract is taken from Luff, I. 'Creating Progress', *Teaching History*, December 2003, 32–33. Reproduced with permission from the Historical Association.

Activities designed primarily to develop an understanding of context

Breakthrough in the West

Rationale

So Hitler was at the Channel in 1940. Well, what about explaining how? So often this crucial contextual consideration is neglected and consequently pupils are expected to make judgements on sources about the ensuing Battle of Britain, the Home Guard or the Blitz without any real concept of the threat posed by the superbly equipped, audacious and well-organised German army. Hitler's victory in France in 1940 ranks as one of the greatest (if not the greatest) military victories of all time. This activity attempts, in a ten minute reconstruction, to demonstrate to pupils just how formidable that army was, and, more importantly for the examination, why Britain's success at preventing that army from landing in Southern England was so important for the outcome of the Second World War.

Level:

GCSE (Modern World)

Assessment Objective:

AO2: 'use historical sources *critically in their context*, by *comprehending*, analysing evaluating and interpreting them'.

Method

1. Arrange the room with three desks pulled together across the front of the classroom on the side furthest from the door. Sit six pupils behind the desks facing the main bulk of the classroom area with backs to the board. Instruct them to assume a casual, overconfident air. This is the Maginot Line. Push all other desks and chairs as far towards the back of the room as possible. Next to the Maginot Line place three large cardboard boxes, bean bags or any soft large obstacle. This is the Ardennes Forest. Behind these place a pupil from your class made scruffy by pulling shirt out and by placing tie over left shoulder – he or she represents General Corap and his execrable troops placed there for safety behind a seemingly impenetrable forest.
2. Take five pupils and place them next to Corap explaining that these French and British troops are on the Belgian border. Ideally, these should be near the classroom door. If your door is elsewhere then pin up a sheet of paper marked 'Dunkirk' near to them.
3. Place five more pupils two metres away from the French/British troops facing them. These are the German forces facing Belgium.
4. Place five more pupils facing the Maginot Line. These again are German troops.

5. Then take the remaining five or six pupils and instruct them to crouch down opposite the 'Ardennes'. These are the new secret German Panzer Divisions.

6. Talk your class through the action conducting them as an orchestra. Tell them that they are to be taken and talked through once then they will be merely gestured through, before finally running the whole action themselves from memory.

7. Move them as follows.

   a) The Germans opposite France and Belgium are to move one metre forward then stop. The French and British troops on the Belgian border advance to meet them, confident of renewed trench warfare in Belgium. They stand almost nose to nose with the Germans.

   b) The Germans opposite the Maginot Line advance half heartedly and thumb their noses at the French seated behind the line who respond by casually pretending to shoot in an unconcerned manner.

   c) At a shout of 'Now' the crouching Panzer divisions shuffle rapidly towards the forest pushing the soft obstacle out of the way and causing the hapless Corap to flee. On Corap's flight, half of the Panzer troops stand behind the British and French in Belgium sandwiching them with the other German troops coming through Belgium.

   d) The other half of the Panzer troops go behind the Maginot Line and shout 'hands up'. The line, unable to turn, obliges.

   e) The sandwiched British and French troops exit through the nearby classroom door – Dunkirk! British first, then French.

8. Perform the action twice more directing less each time. Then debrief in role. Who do you French blame for the defeat? What is the British point of view? How far was the German plan and the modern army responsible for victory? The power of the debrief in role has been demonstrated by Dale Banham and Ian Dawson. It will work here.

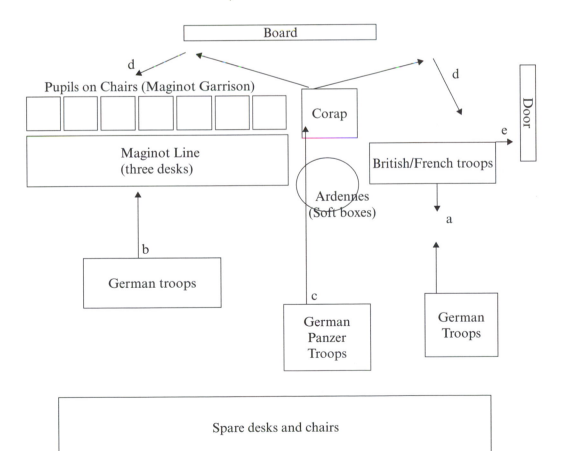

High ability or potential – a history checklist

Quality	1 – Very Strong	2	3	4	5 – Very Weak
Use appropriate examples in their work – to illustrate a depth of understanding or to show understanding and links outside the immediate context of what they are studying					
Show the interconnection and relationship between the events being studied					
Break down historical interpretations and think about the validity and reasonableness of such views					
Place historical sources and interpretations into a historical context – especially in describing how such material was produced or constructed					
Communicate their ideas fluently, not just in the written form, showing balance and a sound conclusion					
Have good general knowledge about the past					
Make independent study of the past					
Show interest in and sensitivity to the past					
Show insight into the past					
Demonstrate skills in group work					
Express emotions easily					
Demonstrate originality and persistence in problem solving					
Are curious					
Attracted to the unusual, the complex and mysterious					
The following characteristics **might** indicate high ability but need to be treated with great caution:					
Stubbornness					
Low interest in details and indifference to some common conventions and courtesies					
Disorganised and sloppy about matters which appear unimportant					
Temperamental, demanding and emotional					
Thought of as 'clever' by their peers					
A potential leader of their peers					

 From *Meeting the Needs of Your Most Able Pupils: History*, Routledge 2007

Vocabulary for framing learning objectives and expected learning outcomes

From Key Stage 3 National Strategy – *Assessment for Learning Whole School Training Materials* – Unit 3: Objective Led Lessons

Draw	State	Record	Recognise	Identify
Sort	Describe	Select	Present	Locate information from text
Decide	Discuss	Define	Classify	Explain how
Devise	Calculate	Interpret	Construct	Clarify
Plan	Predict	Conclude	Solve	Determine the key points from
Formulate	Explain why	Use the pattern to	Reorganise	Explain the differences between
Link/make connections between	Use the idea of ... to ...	Use a model of ... to ...	Provide evidence for	Evaluate the evidence for

Increasing demand (vertical arrow pointing down on left of table)

A community of enquiry on the Norman Conquest

On 5 January 1066 Edward the Confessor – King of England – died with no children. A difficult decision had to be made by the Witan – the ruling council of England – on who should be King next. It was a difficult decision to make. They decided to ask **Harold Godwineson** to be King of England. Harold was the son of the Earl of Wessex – the most powerful nobleman in England. His sister was the wife of Edward the Confessor – the Queen of England. Additionally Harold said that Edward had named him as King just before his death.

There were no rules about who should be made King at the time. Instead the Witan could have chosen **William of Normandy**.

William said he had visited England in 1051 and Edward had promised the throne to him then. Edward had grown up in Normandy and had many Norman friends. He also said that **Harold** had been shipwrecked in Normandy in 1064. Harold had been going there to pay a ransom to rescue his nephew. **William** helped him but he made **Harold** make an oath on holy relics of Saint-Valery that when **Edward** died he would let **William** be King.

A third choice could have been **Harald Hardraada**. Harald was king of Norway. He was a direct descendent of **King Canute**. There were a lot of Viking families in the north of England who might support him. **Harald** also had the support of **Tostig** who was the half brother of **Harold Godwineson**.

There were also other people who could make a claim – but their claims were not so strong.

In September 1066 **Tostig** attacked the Isle of Wight and so **Harold Godwineson** defended the South Coast of England with his army. On September 18 **Harald Hardraada** and his army landed in Yorkshire. **Harold Godwineson** marched his army north and defeated **Hardraada's** troops at Stamford Bridge. **William** had been stuck in Normandy unable to move because of the direction of the wind. Then his luck changed and he was able to set sail with his army to England. He landed near Hastings on September 28.

Harold Godwineson marched his army south. When he arrived at Hastings his troops were tired. Some troops had deserted and left him. He fought the **Battle of Hastings** on October 14 1066. At the beginning of the battle Harold placed his troops at the top of a hill – **Senlac Hill.** Try as they might William and his troops could not break through the Saxon shield wall. William then tried a trick – he got some of his troops on horses to pretend to run away. Harold's troops followed the Normans. The Normans turned around and charged. The Saxon army was broken up. In the confusion **Harold** was killed. **William** had won. Later William built an abbey at the battle site to celebrate and give thanks to God for his victory.

Thinking points:

- Why do you think the Witan chose **Harold Godwineson** to be King?
- What do you think might have happened if the Witan had not chosen **Harold Godwineson** to be King?
- Why might it have been a mistake for **Harold** to fight **Hardraada** in the north?
- Do you think **William** was just lucky?
- Why do you think **William** told the story about the oath that **Harold** took and why do you think he built the abbey?
- What might this story tell us about what it meant to be a medieval King?
- What do you think this story tells us about how people in the Middle Ages thought about God?

From *Meeting the Needs of Your Most Able Pupils: History*, Routledge 2007

Mystery example

A mystery is a particularly powerful kind of problem solving activity. In it pupils are invited – in groups – to answer an enquiry question. To answer this question they must examine a large amount of information. This information can be contradictory, contain red herrings, make inferences and different connections. Pupils enjoy this activity and it works really well.

Why didn't Mr Higgins' men die of cholera?

1. There was a cholera outbreak in England in August 1854.	2. Mr Higgins sought the advice of a quack.
3. People thought the disease was caused by bad air.	4. A quack could give out all sorts of tonics and herbs.
5. It smells badly in a brewery – yeast, sugar and steam.	6. Mr Higgins' brewery was located at Broad Street in Soho, London.
7. Mr Higgins ordered sweet smelling incense to be burnt in his brewery.	8. Jon Snow was the local doctor to Broad Street.
9. There were cholera outbreaks in England in 1831–2, 1848–9, 1854, 1865–6.	10. Jon Snow plotted the deaths in Soho due to cholera.
11. In 1866 a Sanitary Act was passed in England that compelled local authorities to take action on sewerage, water and street cleaning and also smoke, overcrowding and infection.	12. There were lots of deaths near the Broad Street pump.
13. The brewery had its own well.	14. You have to boil water to make beer.
15. People stopped dying of cholera at Broad Street when the water pump handle was replaced.	16. People thought that overcrowding and loose morals caused disease.
17. Cholera causes fever, vomiting and explosive diarrhoea in the victim.	18. People thought the disease was airborne.
19. The Broad Street pump water pipe lay near where people dumped their sewerage.	20. The Broad Street pump was cracked.
21. Jon Snow found that there were a large numbers of deaths from cholera near the Broad Street pump.	22. After the 1854 cholera outbreak, the *Report of the Committee for Scientific Enquiry into the Recent Cholera Outbreak* stated that the body of evidence suggested that cholera was caused by bad air and stink rather than by contaminated water.
23. Louis Pasteur discovered the germ theory in 1861.	

 From *Meeting the Needs of Your Most Able Pupils: History*, Routledge 2007

Lesson structure example using formative assessment strategies

From the GCSE unit, *South Africa since 1948 – a study in depth*

Starter Activity:

I.S.M. of the Soweto riots in 1976 – Pupils recreate this as a 'freeze frame' activity. Pupils are asked to consider how the people involved in the image are feeling. They are asked to consider why the photographer has captured that particular image – what impact is the photographer trying to achieve on the individual? The pupils are also asked to consider what tensions have arisen to create this kind of image? They are asked to speculate what else might be happening out of camera shot. Finally they are asked to consider how significant this is – what might the impact be on a country and its history?

> Starter activates pupil thinking in terms of the affective domain, and the significance of the event. Speculation, at this point, can create access as can a mixture of kinaesthetic and visual learning styles.

Key Question and Learning Objectives:

Pupils are faced with this question:

Where were the highs and lows of Apartheid between 1950 and 1994?

To answer this question pupils will learn to:

- Determine the significance of events in a particular historical period.
- Determine the different relative significance of events in a historical period.
- Explore the impact of different events on peoples' lives.

> A sound historical key question. The learning objectives map out the kind of thinking that will be necessary to answer the key question. The objectives are content free and allude to a set of thinking that is wider than one task. It builds up the plenary session. The teacher simply has to ask how did we determine relative significance etc.

The teacher then tells the pupils what they will do and places the lesson in a historical context. They will:

- Produce a sequenced life line of apartheid.
- Show how apartheid affected two groups of people between 1950 and 1994.
- Annotate the lifeline to show where the most significant events were.

Success Criteria:

- All events will be plotted.

- The lifeline will clearly show which events were the most significant or drastic.

- The lifeline will clearly show why some events are more important than others

The teacher then models the process of how to construct a lifeline by using an analogous example.

Pupils work collaboratively in groups engaged in the task. At a mid point in the lesson they look at each other's work. Using Post-it notes they leave messages for their fellow pupils – about what they like, what they need to do to improve and what they need to think about further.

At the end of the lesson there is a plenary – Some groups display their work and explain how and why they have reached that viewpoint. The teacher then builds the plenary around the objectives by asking the pupils:

- How did they determine the significance of events?

- How did they work out the importance of events when compared to one another?

- Explore the impact of different events on peoples' lives.

- How did they decide where the turning points were?

- Which objectives did they find easier and which did they find more difficult?

> Two strategies could be used – plotting the impact of each individual event in turn and checking the relative distance between different events. Success criteria give an eye for quality rather than act as a mark scheme.

> Not marking or giving grades but qualitative feedback for next steps.

> More of a discussion rather than an activity – but evaluation of learning and making explicit what they have learnt, found easy and found difficult by doing the activity.

References

Arthur, J. and Phillips, P. (ed.) (2000) *Issues in History Teaching*. London: Routledge.

Black, P. and William, D. (1998) *Inside the Black Box*. London: King's College.

Black, P. *et al.* (2003) *Assessment for Learning – Putting it in Practice*. Buckingham: Open University Press.

Bloom, B. (ed.) (1956) *Taxonomy of Educational Objectives*. New York: Longmans, Green & Co.

Byrom, J. *et al.* (1999) *Modern Minds*. London: Longman.

Byrom, J. and Riley, M. (2003) 'Professional wrestling in the history department: a case study in planning the teaching of the British Empire at Key Stage 3', *Teaching History*, **112**, 6–15.

Clark, C. and Callow, R. (2002) *Educating the Gifted & Talented Child*. London: NACE/Fulton.

Clarke, S. (2005) *Formative Assessment in the Secondary Classroom*. London: Hodder Murray.

Counsell, C. (2004) *History and Literacy in Year 7 (History in Practice)*. London: Hodder Murray.

Culpin, C. (1999) 'No puzzle, no learning: how to make your site visits rigorous, fascinating and indispensable', *Teaching History*, **97**, 29–36.

Culpin, C. (2000) *South Africa since 1948*. London: John Murray.

Davies, P., Lynch, D. and Davies, R. (2003) *Enlivening Secondary History*. London: Routledge Falmer.

Department for Education and Skills (1997) *Excellence in Schools*. London: DfES.

Dweck, C. S. (1999) *Self Theories – Their Role in Motivation, Personality and Development*. Philadelphia: Psychology Press.

Evans, G. R. (2002) *Faith in the Medieval World*. London: Lion Publishing.

Ferguson, N. (2003) *Virtual History*. London: Pan.

Fisher, P. (2002) *Thinking Through History*. Cambridge: Chris Kingston Publishing.

Fisher, R. (2003) *Teaching Thinking*, 2nd edn. London: Continuum Publishing.

Fullan, M. (2001) *The New Meaning of Educational Change*. New York: Teachers College Press.

Gabler, I. C. and Schroeder, M. (2003) *Constructivist Methods for the Secondary Classroom – Engaged Minds*. New York: Allyn Bacon.

Gardner, H. (1983) *Frames of Mind*. London: Fontana Press.

Gardner, H. (2004) *The Unschooled Mind – How Children Think and How Schools Should Teach*. New York: Basic Books.

George, D. (1997) *The Challenge of the Second Child*, 2nd edn. London: David Fulton Publishers.

Ginnis, P. (2002) *The Teacher's Toolkit*. Carmarthen: Crown House Publishing.

Harris, A., Day, C., Hopkins, D., Ellison, L. and Hadfield, M. (2003) *Effective Leadership for School Improvement*. London: Routledge Falmer.

Harris, R. (2005) 'Does differentiation have to mean different?', *Teaching History*, **118**, 5–13.

Hawthorn, G. (1991) *Plausible Worlds – Possibility and Understanding in History and the Social Sciences*. Cambridge: CUP.

Haydn, T. and Counsell, C. (eds) (2003) *History, ICT and Learning in the Secondary School*. London: Routledge Falmer.

Hedger, K. and Jesson, D. (1998) *The Numbers Game: Using Assessment Data in Schools*. London: Centre for Performance and Resource Management.

Hopkins, D., Harris, A. *et al.* (2000) *Creating the Conditions for Teaching and Learning*. London: David Fulton Publishers.

Hymer, B. and Michel, D. (2002) *Gifted & Talented Learners – Creating a Policy for Inclusion*. London: David Fulton Publishers.

Joyce, B., Calhoun, E. and Hopkins, D. (2002) *Models of Learning – Tools for Teaching*, 2nd ed. Buckingham: Open University Press.

Joyce, B. and Showers, B. (2002) *Raising Students' Achievement Through Staff Development*, 3rd ed. Alexandra VA USA: Association for Supervision and Curriculum Development.

Key Stage 3 National Strategy (2002) *Training Material for the Foundation Subjects* (especially modules 4, 7, 8, 9, 12, 13). London: HMSO.

Key Stage 3 National Strategy (2003) *Sustaining Improvement: A Suite of Modules on Coaching, Networking and Capacity Building*. London: HMSO.

Key Stage 3 National Strategy (2004) *Assessment for Learning Whole School Training Materials*. London: HMSO.

Lipman, M. (2003) *Thinking in Education*, 2nd edn. Cambridge: CUP.

Lomas, T. (1990) *Teaching and Assessing Historical Understanding*. London: Historical Association.

Marwick, A. (2001) *The New Nature of History – Knowledge, Evidence and Language*. London: Palgrave Macmillan.

Montgomery, D. (2003) *Gifted & Talented Children with Special Educational Needs – Double Exceptionality*. London: NACE/David Fulton Publishers.

National Advisory Committee on Creative and Cultural Education (NACCCE) (1999) *All Our Futures: Creativity, Culture and Education*.

National College for School Leadership (2005) *Leading Coaching in Schools – Leading Practice Seminar Series*.

Ofsted (2003) *Handbook for Inspecting Secondary Schools*. London: Ofsted.

Ofsted (2003) *Inspection of Local Education Authorities; Ofsted/Audit Commission Inspection Guidance*. December 2003 v1a. London: Ofsted.

Phillips, R. (2002) *Reflective Teaching of History, 11–18*. London: Continuum Publishing.

Rudd, P., Rickinson, M. and Benefield, P. (2004) *Mapping Work on the Future of Teaching and Learning*, Final Report to the General Teaching Council. London: NfER.

Stemberg, R. J. (1997) *Thinking Styles*. Cambridge: CUP.

Stoll, L. *et al.* (2003) *It's about learning (and it's about time!) What's in it for schools?* London: Routledge Falmer.

Taylor, R. (2003) *How to Read a Church.* London: Rider and Co.

Teaching History (2004) 'Assessment without levels?', **115**. London: Historical Association.

Torrance, P. (1977) *Discovering and Nurturing of Giftedness in the Culturally Different.* Reston VA: Council for Exceptional Children.

Torrance, P. (1980) 'Assessing the further reaches of creative potential' , *Journal of Creative Behaviour*, **14**, 1–19.

Watkin, N. and Ahrenfelt, J. (2005) 'Mixing a G and T cocktail: teaching about heritage through a cross-curricular enquiry', *Teaching History – Rethinking Differentiation*, **118**.

White, H. (1974) *Metahistory: Historical Imagination in Nineteenth Century Europe.* Baltimore: John Hopkins University Press.

Wragg, E. C. and Brown, G. (2001) *Questioning in the Secondary School.* London: Routledge Falmer.